Islam in Egypt Today

Social and Political Aspects of Popular Religion

MORROE BERGER

Professor of Sociology
Princeton University

CAMBRIDGE
At the University Press
1970

Published by the Syndics of the Cambridge University Press
Bentley House, 200 Euston Road, London N.W.1
American Branch: 32 East 57th Street, New York, N.Y.10022

Library of Congress Catalogue Card Number: 70–113597

Standard Book Number: 521 07834 2

Printed in Great Britain
at the University Printing House, Cambridge
(Brooke Crutchley, University Printer)

Islam in Egypt Today

This volume is one of a series:

PRINCETON STUDIES ON THE NEAR EAST

For information, write to Program in
Near Eastern Studies, Princeton University,
Princeton, New Jersey, U.S.A. 08540

Contents

To the People of Egypt

Preface

I had intended to give the subjects of this book more field study before writing on them. Various uncertainties, however, have persuaded me to offer this report now in order to provide information on several aspects of religious behavior and organization in Egypt today.

It is a pleasure to record my thanks to those who have helped me. For general guidance I am indebted to Dr Muhammed El Bahay, former Minister of Waqfs, and to Dr Ibrahim Madkour, Secretary General of the Academy of the Arabic Language. I received much practical advice from H. E. Salah Dessouki, former Governor of Cairo. Professor Bernard Lewis, of the School of Oriental and African Studies in the University of London, read an early draft. For indispensable advice in the day-to-day research, I am deeply indebted to Mr Labib al-Said, of the Ministry of Waqfs, and to Mr Fathi Osman formerly of that Ministry. In studying sufi organization, I received much help from Shaikh Muhammad Ulwan, the head of the federation of sufi orders. Of course, I am alone responsible for the use to which I have, in this book, put the suggestions of these scholars and statesmen. I want again to acknowledge the continued help, for over a quarter of a century, of my friend Mr Z. Misketian. Finally, I must mention the cooperation I have always received from many other people (friends and subjects of study) in Egypt; the dedication of this volume is only a weak indication of my debt to the many Egyptians I have met while living and studying there.

The opportunity to spend a year in Egypt to make this study was provided by the United States Office of Education through a Fulbright–Hays fellowship. The Program in Near Eastern Studies at Princeton University has provided general support of various kinds for this study as well as for others over many years.

MORROE BERGER

vii

Note on Transliteration and References

Arabic words or names familiar in other languages are left in their usual English form. Others are transliterated consistently in a way conforming (with few exceptions) to most systems.

Footnote references to sources are brief, directing the reader to the List of Sources at the end of the book, where full citations are given.

1

Islamic government and voluntary associations

The trend toward secularization in the Islamic Middle East in this century has meant a decline not only in the overt influence of religious ideas and organizations upon social and political life but also a decline in the attention scholars have been willing to give to contemporary religion. Just as the Middle East governments have done, so scholars have emphasized the more obvious aspects of nationalism, industrialization, agrarian reform, as well as the secular means of mobilizing public opinion. These governments and scholars have also, from time to time, assured us that Islam continues to be important, but the former have gone on using and weakening religion, and the latter have hardly moved beyond nineteenth-century reformist ideas. As a result, there is not enough information about contemporary religious institutions and associations in the Islamic Middle East, and the deeper aspects of social life have escaped observation.

The purpose of this study is, therefore, twofold. First, it aims to provide information about several aspects of religious behavior and organization in Egypt today. The data presented come from several Egyptian governmental studies virtually unknown beyond official circles, interviews with religious leaders, and observation of religious activities. Some of this material offers elementary facts about religion, for the scholarly neglect has continued so long that such facts are now needed. The personal observations reported here were made mainly in 1964–5 but are based on several years of study in Egypt before and since then. Second, this book aims to stimulate scholarly interest in religious behavior in the Islamic Middle East.

To achieve these goals, I discuss four broad subjects. First, I consider briefly the nature of government and of voluntary association in Islamic societies, and conclude that both doctrine and practice have been more hospitable to voluntary association than traditional Western accounts have indicated. Second, I describe some aspects of religious institutions in Egypt today, including mosque organization and governmental efforts to use religion for its own purposes. Third, I take up some aspects of sufi organization today. Finally, I describe and analyze the Egyptian voluntary religious associations (jamʿīyāt dīnīya or khairīya) engaging in educational, charitable, and other welfare activities. I want to emphasize that I am not trying to give here a full or even balanced picture of popular religion or the religious establishment. I am trying only to report some facets of religious behavior and organization that I have been able to observe, and to give some background concerning these subjects. The result is that the particular points I discuss may not be always clearly related to one another and may not be the ones that all readers will regard as most significant or interesting. Finally, I have not been able to offer documentary evidence for everything I report, for in a society like Egypt much of great importance does not receive expression in that form. I can only hope that in such cases the evidence of my own observation and what people have told me will ultimately receive corroboration both in the experience of other observers and in documents as well.

The familiar statement that Islam is a religion, a culture, and a polity is no doubt illuminating, but it also conceals the diversity that has accompanied this integrative tendency. A brief examination of the Islamic ideas of God and His law and of the Muslim community and its sovereign (Allah and shari'a, umma and khilāfa or imamate) shows how doctrine has given to voluntary associations a place which they have managed to occupy despite the inclination of governments to reduce it.

Allah is of course the prime mover, the source and creator of all things, including the other three elements. Through his Messenger, Muhammad, Allah provided the Koran, the basis of the shari'a, containing the duties men must perform in order to reach Paradise. The shari'a was thus not only a constitutional system but an ideal of conduct to be followed by Muslims and a legal code dealing with everyday life. The community of Muslims, the umma, owed loyalty first to Allah and then to the shari'a. The umma was at its creation a religious community guided by Muhammad under the direction of Allah. Upon the Messenger's death, a group of the faithful acting for the umma chose a successor to him, the caliph (khalīfa or imam), whose function was to facilitate the efforts of the believers to reach Paradise and to protect them as a community. In return, the umma must obey the caliph, but this loyalty to a state-like instrumentality was clearly separate from and secondary to the umma's loyalty to Allah and the law. The state is thus not itself one of the fundamental elements in the building of Islamic society but emerges through the institution of the caliphate (khilāfa) and then makes increasingly wide claims to obedience as a necessity for the protection of the umma. Although later jurists found Koranic support for the notion of absolute obedience to the caliph, whose authority was held to come from Allah, no amount of exegesis has been able to convince the umma at all times and in all places that it must never challenge the caliph's combination of religious and temporal power. Islam inculcated among the believers a strong sense of solidarity (and perhaps even of uniformity) to discourage deviation;

yet at the same time Islamic doctrine and practice have conveyed an equally strong sense of free association among believers to achieve the common goals of right individual conduct on earth. In the absence of a system of complete regulation by the official bureaucratic religion, the popular religion was able to develop broad and enduring associational ties on a different level.[1]

It is possible that both the emphasis upon solidarity and the disposition to independent association in Islam stem partly from its early relation to nomadic tribesmen. The effort to convert and retain the loyalty of members of these autonomous communities so suspicious of outside influences demanded discipline and centralized power. This necessity may account for the stress, in the Koran and traditions, upon unity and constraint, and upon what scholars have taken to be an identity of religious, moral and state powers. Yet the conversion of the tribes brought into Islam a group that was hostile to centralized power, a group in which non-specialized agencies performed those functions which in settled communities were carried out by more specialized agencies of the state. By their very stubbornness, nomadic communities inspire severity in those who would govern them; at the same time their mode of life calls for pervasive and constant cooperation among themselves even though there is no state apparatus as such.

This associative injunction and propensity is reflected in the many uses, both religious and secular, of the root jmʿ, to gather, to combine. It is one of the most fruitful roots in a language known for its capacity for ramification. All of the following forms convey some sense of people coming together: jamāʿa, majmaʿ, jāmiʿ, jamʿ, jamʿīya, mujtamaʿ. Over

---

[1] This distinction between official and popular religion has been made often; see Weber, p. 90. On the terms Allah, sharīʿa, umma, and khilāfa, see the chapters by H. A. R. Gibb and Joseph Schacht in Khadduri and Liebesny, and Sanhouri, Chapter 1.

the centuries these and other derivations have been sorted out as to their meanings, some of them after going through considerable change.[1]

The first of these words, jamā'a, very early in Islam came to mean the community of Muslims as in al-jamā'a al-islāmīya, or the community of believers as in al-jamā'a al-mu'minīn. A similar term, ahl al-sunna wa-l jamā'a refers to the orthodox Islamic community. The ṣalāt al-jamā'a is collective prayer (prayer of the gathering) in the mosque, which is preferred to individual prayer. Another form, ijmā', refers to the agreement (the coming together) of the jamā'a or of the authorities on a legal matter. The word jum'a, meaning both week and Friday (the day of the gathering), has a religious and a secular (reputedly pre-Islamic) meaning. It is used also in a phrase meaning the collective Friday prayer: ṣalāt al-jum'a. Another religious context is supplied to the word jāmi', meaning comprehensive, or one that gathers; al-masjid al-jāmi' thus became the regional central mosque where Muslims gather for the Friday prayer, and later jāmi' itself acquired this meaning. In the nineteenth century jāmi'a, meaning an association of disparate elements with a common interest, was introduced for the European term university, that is, what we today call an aggregation of schools covering most of man's knowledge.

Until the nineteenth century, the word jam'īya, meaning association, meeting, or assembly, was used to refer to society in general, or, for example, to European or Muslim society. Ibn Khaldun used the related word, ijtimā', for this purpose, as in al-ijtimā' al-insāni, human society. In the last century, however, jam'īya began to acquire a narrower meaning, that of a club or association for a specific purpose, such as the

---

[1] On the root jm' see Wehr; Ibn Manẓūr, Volume 9; article on Masdjid in *Shorter E.I.*, pp. 336*a*, 336*b*, 337*b*; and the following articles in *E.I.*²: Djamā'a, Djāmi'a, Djam'iyya, Djum'a. In briefly examining this subject, I have had access to reports of the Academy of the Arabic Language in Cairo through its Secretary General, Dr Ibrahim Madkour.

pursuit of science or literature or some activity for the welfare of the community in a secular sense. At the same time, mujtama', meaning place of gathering, replaced jam'īya in the sense of society in general. Today jam'īya means a voluntary benevolent society of the sort discussed in Chapter 4.

A Muslim scholar has recently argued that the word īmān, usually taken to mean belief, has the additional meaning of causing someone to feel secure from danger. He asserts that several Koranic verses suggest this meaning in the historical context of the rise of Islam. When he adopted Islam, a man lost the security of the Arab tribe and its gods; the security of association with other Muslims was offered in its place: 'īmān is this idea of "associating oneself with, or enrollment in the group of the monotheists," thus assuring oneself security... Thus the problem was association or dissociation, joining or quitting, supporting or rejecting, in an age of socio-political grouping and formation of alliances for the very essential need of survival.'[1]

In carrying out their duties, as individuals and as a community, Muslims have from the beginning combined in organizations outside the state. They have often, moreover, acted as if they believed it did not matter what the state did so long as it did not prevent the believers from obeying the rules of conduct prescribed by Allah. They combined in guilds, young men's associations, secret societies, mystical religious orders, and benevolent associations; they also adopted an instrument for charitable purposes, the waqf, by which (with other voluntary means) they supported mosques. The Muslim's sense of individual responsibility and individual salvation has impelled him to join with others in the effort to fulfill the numerous and detailed requirements of so comprehensive a system of religious law as represented in the sharī'a.

[1] Abdul Rauf, pp. 96, 98–9.

Islamic government

The contemporary religious institutions and associations of Egypt are the main subjects of this study; at this point, therefore, it will be useful to mention briefly the examples of voluntary activity in the upkeep of mosques and in the waqf, and to refer to medieval and early modern urban associations that have been studied recently.

The mosque was the first place in which Muslims gathered, for religious and political purposes. Despite this early conjunction, which accentuated governmental functions and powers, mosques nevertheless afforded scope for voluntary activity by the community. Many of the earliest ones were built and maintained with private funds, and such practice has continued on a substantial scale down to the present day. For more than a millennium the chief instrument by which mosques have been supported by private funds has been the waqf, which confers the right to use the fruits of property without transferring ownership. Muslims extended the waqf to all kinds of voluntary charitable purposes.[1]

Gabriel Baer's analysis of *Egyptian Guilds in Modern Times*[2] shows the tension between the desire of the associations to be free and the desire of governments to control them. Ottoman rulers took over the guilds in order to control them more effectively, so that ultimately the leaders of the guilds became instruments by which governments managed the members rather than means by which members could remain autonomous in important matters. This pattern of development has been repeated in the sufi orders and the benevolent societies, as Chapters 3 and 4 will show.

Lapidus has summarized and interpreted a vast amount of data on associational life in Damascus, Aleppo, and Cairo during Mamluk rule from the thirteenth to the sixteenth cen-

---

[1] On mosques, see article on Masdjid, *Shorter E.I.*, pp. 348–50, and Gibb and Bowen, p. 165. On waqf, see Henry Cattan's chapter in Khadduri and Liebesny.
[2] Baer 1964, pp. 31–2, 42–3, 77–9, 125–6.

turies A.D. Although the 'military system,' he shows, 'towered over the subject societies in power and wealth,' nevertheless the people built their own 'stable social and religious life which preserved their integrity...' The religious communities, in particular, were never 'entirely subordinate' to the claims of the state though the 'consolidation of the faith owed much' to its support. These urban communities were given some cohesion through the leadership of the religious officials ('ulamā), who were 'an administrative and social as well as a religious elite.' Both the Mamluk rulers and the religious officials were highly suspicious of associations. The rulers regarded them as 'parapolitical' irrespective of their origins, while the religious leaders feared them as divisive of the umma and as 'sources of heresy.'[1] In recent years political and religious leaders in Egypt have held similar attitudes toward voluntary associations. The leaders of the religious and secular associations today, like those in earlier eras,[2] thus stand equivocally between the rulers and the ruled, now controlling the association in the interest of the former, now preserving it in at least some form in the interest of the latter.

There is, however, no doubt that with increasing secularization and the growing state monopoly of authority and power, the voluntary associations have lost the autonomy that earlier doctrine and practice permitted. Sanhoury, like others, pointed out that the Prophet founded a religion and a state at the same time. 'But,' he added, 'his main goal was, above everything, to found the religion. The founding of the state was only secondary.'[3] This ancillary power has become the chief one; its doctrine and practice do not afford even the ambiguity of the system it has displaced, so that free associational life is steadily declining.

[1] Lapidus, pp. 6–7, 107–8, 103–4.
[2] See Gibb and Bowen, pp. 110–12, for a similar characterization regarding the eighteenth century.
[3] Sanhoury, p. 266.

2

Religious organization: the mosque and governmental policy

Despite changes in modern times, much of the religious life of Muslims is still centered around the mosque, and religion as an institution of social control is still centered on governmental agencies. Mosque and government are still connected but each is changing. The persisting distinction between them may be seen in two facts: in the first place, many mosques continue to be somewhat independent of the governmental religious establishment; and in the second, it is still valid to distinguish between the religious officials ('ulamā) whose functions are in the mosque, that is, who are concerned with worship and preaching, and those whose functions relate to doctrine, religious law, and central administration through governmental agencies. The connection between mosque and government may be seen in the fact that both the mosque and the doctrinal and administrative 'ulamā are still based upon sacred learning ('ilm). As the secular government increases its power over religious organizations (especially in the domains of justice and education—courts and schools) these connections between popular religious agencies and the governmental religious establishment grow, and the power of the 'ulamā declines.

THE MOSQUE

Mosques in Egypt today are established and maintained by private individuals or associations of private individuals, and the government as represented by the Ministry of Waqfs. All mosques, irrespective of their origin and maintenance, are subject to governmental inspection. A department of the Ministry of Waqfs inspects the administration of the mosque to see if the officials and employees carry out their duties. The Ministry of Public Health inspects the sanitary facilities (including water supply and plumbing fixtures); if it finds them substandard, the mosque administration must correct the deficiencies.

Most mosques have at least three of the following officials.[1] The chief official of the mosque is the imam, who is also the leader in public prayer. If the mosque is a small one, he is usually the khatīb too, the one who gives the sermon during the Friday noon public prayer. In such mosques he is also likely to be the qāṣṣ or wā'iz, the one who preaches moral lessons daily except Friday between the maghrib prayer (around sunset) and the 'ishā (at night). For governmental mosques, the Ministry of Waqfs selects imams from among the graduates of the various faculties of Al-Azhar University. The most highly qualified imams are the graduates of the faculty of theology (uṣul al-dīn). Since the need for imams is greater than the number of these graduates, the Ministry often assigns to smaller mosques imams who have completed only the Al-Azhar secondary school level. Private mosques have often had to take on imams with less formal training. Most imams in these mosques have failed to obtain the diploma in one or another section of Al-Azhar. Others, rather older, received good training in an Al-Azhar institute, no longer in existence, which had a position between the secondary school and the advanced faculties. According to some observers, the general level of religious training of imams has declined in the last decade or so. The pay of imams in government mosques is higher than the pay of those in

[1] These posts have not changed much over the centuries. See article on Masdjid, *Shorter E.I.*; Gibb and Bowen, p. 96; Zwemer, p. 60.

private mosques. The former receive about twenty to ninety Egyptian pounds monthly, depending upon grade, while the latter receive far less.

The muezzin (mu'adhdhin), or caller to prayer, once needed only a good voice. In 1962 he was required to have a certificate of graduation from an Al-Azhar secondary school, but few practicing muezzins have it as yet. In the smaller mosques the muezzin usually acts for the imam in his absence.

Large mosques have an overseer (mulāḥiẓ). Under the direction of the imam, he is the chief administrative official, the keeper of the keys; he supervises the other employees and is responsible for cleanliness, water supply and the physical upkeep of the mosque.

Most mosques have at least one servant (khādim), who cleans and guards the mosque. In very small mosques, one man is often both muezzin and servant. Today even the servant must have some religious qualifications; he is supposed to know by heart one section (juz') of the thirty sections into which the Koran is divided.

In 1962 a new mosque post was created, the mosque attendant (muqīm al-shaʿāʾir), to assist in religious ceremonies.[1] This official combines the function of muezzin with some other duties such as chanting the Koran on Fridays and administering the library if there is one. The new post has not taken hold. People still speak of the muezzin no matter what other duties he may have; even small mosques need an official who can satisfactorily call the faithful to prayer even if he can do nothing else.

There is one post that is not important in the larger affairs involving religion and power but it bears intimately upon the feelings of most Muslims, religious or not. This is the reciter of the Koran (qāriʾ), who performs his duties not only in connection with mosque prayer but also in ceremonies

---

[1] Law No. 97 of 1962; see Ministry of Waqfs 1964*b*, pp. 74, 77.

held in other places. The qāri' must know the Koran by heart and have a good voice. To qualify, a candidate in the provinces must study under a teacher of recitation (muqri'), from whom he obtains a diploma. Al-Azhar also has an institute of recitation (ma'had al-qirā'āt), which gives a diploma after a formal test. Often the reciters from the provinces are superior because they study with great teachers who give their pupils more attention than teachers in the institute do. With the diploma, the reciter is eligible to become a muezzin or a reciter of the Koran before the Friday prayer. Candidates who want the Al-Azhar diploma must sit for an examination by a five-man committee which, when I observed its work, was composed of three venerable Al-Azhar shaikhs, an official of the Ministry of Waqfs, and a secular musical expert who had been the president of the Institute of Arab Music (as well as a highly capable amateur player of oriental music, a judge, and a lay psychologist). The committee met regularly and frequently in the office of the Ministry official, where I observed its procedures many times. The candidates gathered in the corridor, and one was called in at a time. He would remove his shoes and sit cross-legged on a straight-backed chair. The examiners would ask him to recite various passages of the Koran for ten to twenty minutes. Meanwhile, in the oriental manner, the ordinary affairs conducted in the office went on as usual, except that people lowered their voices in deference to the candidate who was reciting in full voice. Over several months, I saw and heard at least twenty-five candidates, most of whom were thirty to thirty-five years old, though a few were in their twenties and some looked around fifty. Many of them had some marked physical disability, and perhaps five of those I saw were blind. The standards were high and the test a rigorous one. Most of the candidates I saw were visibly nervous, but the members of the committee were patient, friendly, and tried to put the candidates at their ease. As soon as a candidate completed the test, he left the room; the judges then wrote their individual decisions, discussed the composite rating they would give, and wrote their report. Of the candidates I saw examined, perhaps a quarter were successful.

The worshippers in the mosque, as distinct from its officials, are not so easily classified. Unlike churches and synagogues, mosques do not have regular 'congregations', nor are the worshippers in a given mosque drawn from the same social class because of the character of the neighborhood. Except for a very few in Western-style suburbs, and of recent origin, mosques do not take on the character of their location. Though a neighborhood may be largely middle-class, for example, the worshippers will include servants, merchants, civil servants, and others. Within the mosque, too, there are no special corners or honored places. Worshippers select a mosque mainly on the basis of proximity to home or place of work; in recent years proximity to home has become more important as Friday has increasingly become the day of rest from work. On special occasions, too, worshippers select a mosque because they admire the preacher of the Friday sermon or the reciter of moralizing stories.

In recent years the Ministry of Waqfs has made two intensive studies of the number and condition of all mosques in the country. These surveys, which I shall summarize and comment upon here, are justly regarded as the first systematic attempts to provide reliable information about mosques as a modern census does about population. Completed in 1963 and 1964, the surveys describe conditions prevailing in 1962. These studies had a precedent of a sort, however, in an attempt in 1942 to persuade the government to adopt a modern and methodical approach to mosque administration. This was a report of the Sanitation Committee for Mosque Improvement, a special advisory committee to the Minister of Waqfs. Although it was concerned mainly with hygiene, the committee recommended a certain rationalization of mosque policies.[1] The report commended the Ministry for its progress in the upkeep of mosques during the previous two decades but felt that the time had come to set forth a clear and enduring policy of reform based upon three principles. First, the mosque should be regarded as a public utility; specific legislation should systematize construction and administration, and the government should contribute financially when the Ministry of Waqfs and private owners are unable to meet expenses. Second, the distribution of mosques throughout the country should meet the public's needs in various districts. Some places have many more mosques per person than others do. The committee suggested that there should be one mosque (with a courtyard of at least 225 square meters) per 5,000 people, and estimated that it would take twenty years of planned restoration and construction to achieve this distribution. To help plan this program, however, it pointed to the need for an accurate and comprehensive survey of all mosques. Finally, the committee recommended that all functions concerning mosques be centralized in the Ministry of Waqfs, which would, however, continue to cooperate with other government agencies such as the Ministry of Public Health.

Upon these three principles the committee based several further suggestions. Apparently disturbed by the appearance and unhygienic condition of mosques not subject to regulation and inspection, it pointed out that a holy place should be clean; the worshippers should understand this point, but the imams and the staff of the mosque had the obligation to insure cleanliness. It then specified the proper condition of each part of the mosque, including the inner courtyard, minaret, sacred ground around the mosque, lavatory, and various

---

[1] Sanitation Committee, *passim*.

rooms. The committee emphasized the need for regular maintenance by a staff suitably paid and at least a monthly inspection. Without waiting for the statistical survey it had just recommended, the committee estimated that the country needed 4,000 mosques. Half that number were in existence (some needing repair), and the other 2,000 should be constructed over the next twenty years at an approximate cost of £E10,000 per mosque, to which must be added an annual maintenance cost of £E250. All this, the committee concluded, was well within the capacity of the state treasury; indeed, the program would lighten the state's other social burdens because the mosque is a wholesome and effective means to make people aware of the importance of health and to promote moral and social improvement.

Something approximating this suggested building program was achieved later on, according to a report on the work of the Ministry of Waqfs during the first twelve years of the 1952 revolution.[1] The Ministry itself built 78 new mosques at a total cost of £E1,417,971, or an average of about £E18,000 for each one. In addition, the Ministry contributed £E1,235,000 toward the completion of 1,560 private mosques. Thus, 1,638 mosques were built in this twelve-year period, compared with the recommendation that 2,000 should be built in the twenty years beginning 1942. A large number of the private mosques (whether or not built with financial aid from the Ministry of Waqfs) have come under the Ministry's administration in accordance with a law of 1960. Eight hundred such mosques were annexed in 1961 and 1962, and 200 more in 1963.[2] In the next few years about 500 mosques were taken over annually but the pace has slowed down since about 1966.

Although a survey of mosques had been recommended in

---

[1] Ministry of Waqfs 1964*b*, p. 73.
[2] Law 157 of 1960; see Ministry of Waqfs 1964*b*, p. 73.

1942, none was undertaken until about twenty years later. Then two comprehensive inquiries were made as part of the general effort to reform religious organization and education, including the entire Al-Azhar system. The first, completed in 1963, covered the 3,006 mosques owned and directly supervised by the government.[1] The second, completed in 1964, covered 14,212 private mosques.[2] The surveys, carried out in late 1962, were made available to a limited audience but their results were mentioned by the Deputy Minister of Waqfs in a published newspaper interview.[3] They give a large amount of statistical information on three main subjects: (1) the mosques: number, age, size, and condition of the buildings and equipment, (2) mosque officials and employees: their training, qualifications, and salaries; (3) the use of mosques: proportion in use and average number of male Muslims per mosque. Many of these data are presented, also, for each geographical division, including the two largest cities of Cairo and Alexandria. I shall sumarize much of this information about the governmental and private mosques and shall compare them where the statistics permit.[4]

The survey defines both types of mosque. Mosques supervised by the Ministry of Waqfs are called 'governmental mosques' and include four kinds. (1) Public mosques (al-masājid al-khairīya) are those originally belonging to the Ministry and whose officials are considered government employees. (2) Mosques established by joint waqfs (awqāf mushtarika), public and private, were administered for a long time by the Ministry, supported by public waqfs, and have become like public mosques in virtually every respect. In the survey they are not differentiated from public mosques.

---

[1] Ministry of Waqfs 1963. [2] Ministry of Waqfs 1964*a*.

[3] *Akhbār al-yawm* (Cairo), 13 April 1968, p. 12.

[4] The methods by which the survey of both types of mosque was made are described in the volume on private mosques: Ministry of Waqfs 1964*a*, pp. xviii–xx (pp. ṣ, q, r, the last three in the introductory section of the report).

(3) Recent mosques (al-masājid al-mustajidda) are those originally supported by private waqfs but since 1953 (Law 247) managed by the Ministry following the abolition of these waqfs in the previous year. (4) Annexed mosques (al-masājid al-maḍmūma) are those over which the Ministry had already taken control in accordance with Law 157 of 1960, which authorized it to assume, within ten years, the administration of all mosques not yet under its supervision. The fifth type of mosque is non-governmental. Private mosques (al-masājid al-ahlīya) are those built by individuals or associations for whatever reason; these mosques are not subject to the same restrictions as are the four previous kinds.[1] I shall call these two types of mosque governmental (hukūmī or khairī), and private (ahlī). The two words khairī and ahlī, as applied to mosques, derive from the two types of traditional waqf or endowment, the one for a public purpose (waqf khairī) and the one for a private, family purpose (waqf ahlī). The distinction between a 'public' and 'private' mosque, however, refers only to its origin and maintenance by the government or by private persons; so far as use of mosques by Muslims is concerned all are 'public' in the sense of being open to everyone. To avoid misunderstanding on this point, I use the terms governmental mosques and private mosques.

Table 1 shows the total number of governmental and private mosques in the various governorates (provinces) in 1962. There were then 3,006 governmental mosques and 14,212 private mosques. The earlier survey of governmental mosques gives only 2,997, of which 1,685 were 'public' mosques, 520 'recent' mosques, and 792 'annexed' mosques.[2]

[1] Ministry of Waqfs 1963, pp. ii-iii (pp. b, j, in the introductory section).
[2] The figure 2,997 and the breakdown shown above are given in Ministry of Waqfs 1963, p. 2. The later survey of private mosques gives nine more governmental mosques, in the New Valley governorate (Ministry of Waqfs 1964a, pp. 1, 75). I use either figur e,depending upon the point and the source under discussion. The difference is negligible.

TABLE 1. *Number of governmental and private mosques in 1962, and number of male Muslims per mosque, by governorate*

Governorate	Number of mosques			No. of male Muslims per mosque[a]
	Govern-mental	Private	Total	
Cairo	523	218	741	2,028
Alexandria[b]	165	209	374	1,895
Port Said	13	27	40	2,901
Ismailiya	14	218	232	593
Suez	11	60	71	1,367
Damietta	77	86	163	1,208
Daqhaliya	287	1,217	1,504	663
Sharqiya	166	1,787	1,953	460
Qalyubiya	114	482	596	827
Kafr al Shaikh	145	632	777	615
Gharbiya	275	759	1,034	808
Minoufiya	140	915	1,055	626
Buhaira	194	835	1,029	796
Giza	77	457	534	1,218
Beni Suef	132	425	557	713
Fayoum	75	575	650	611
Minya	179	871	1,050	600
Assiut	123	782	905	588
Sohag	110	1,983	2,093	318
Qena	101	1,370	1,471	420
Aswan	52	251	303	591
Red Sea	8	6	14	1,052
New Valley[c]	9	30	39	422
Sinai	16	17	33	770
Total	3,006[d]	14,212	17,218	701

[a] Governmental and private mosques in relation to population as recorded in 1960 census.
[b] Includes Western Desert governorate.
[c] Southern Desert governorate.
[d] The usual figure for governmental mosques, on which the survey's calculations are based, is 2,997 (see Ministry of Waqfs 1963, p. 2).

Source: Ministry of Waqfs 1964*a*, table, p. 75.

Thus even though the government added about 1,300 mosques in the decade or so since 1952, private mosques in 1962 remained 83 per cent of the total in the country. Governmental mosques, as table 1 shows, outnumbered private mosques only in Cairo, the capital, which also has a large number of monumental mosques built by rulers and long run by government. Among the other larger regions, Alexandria is the only one where the number of governmental mosques approaches that of the private ones. The governorates are rather dissimilar regions, some, like Cairo and Alexandria, being entirely urban, and others, like the Red Sea and Sinai, being sparsely populated 'frontier' regions. The other governorates contain medium-size cities, villages, and sparsely settled areas. The table also shows the number of male Muslims per mosque. For the entire country, and for both governmental and private mosques combined, the average was 701. Since governmental mosques are far less numerous, the number of male Muslims for each one is greater, totalling 3,992.[1] The more urbanized areas, also, have a higher average number of potential users; for example, Cairo has 2,028, Alexandria 1,895, and Port Said 2,901.

It is interesting to examine the distribution of mosques in those governorates that are neither urban (like Cairo and Alexandria) nor frontier (like Red Sea and Sinai). Of the remaining sixteen governorates, the surveys give certain information for thirteen, which in 1960 included nearly 17 million people, or about two thirds of the total population. This information relates to the mosques in the capital city of the governorate (the bandar), and to the administrative district (markaz) in which the capital city is located. The district of course has a larger area and greater population, but the capital city is more densely populated.[2] The districts generally have more mosques of both kinds (governmental and private) than do the capital cities. This is the case in the fol-

[1] Ministry of Waqfs 1963, p. 82.
[2] The data on the bandar and markaz are extracted from tables in Ministry of Waqfs 1963, pp. 86–98, and in Ministry of Waqfs 1964a, pp. 85–101.

lowing eleven governorates: Buhaira, Gharbiya, Minoufiya, Kafr al Shaikh, Sharqiya, Daqhaliya, Damietta, Fayoum, Sohag, Beni Suef, and Assiut. Only in the Giza and Qalyubiya governorates do the capital cities have more mosques than the districts. Having fewer mosques and a denser population, the capital cities also have a larger number of male Muslims per mosque; in only two governorates, Kafr al Shaikh and Minoufiya, is this not the case.

When, however, we compare the distribution of governmental mosques with that of private mosques, it becomes clear that the former are more likely to predominate in the capital cities. Thus in the following five governorates the capital cities have more governmental mosques than do the districts: Buhaira, Minoufiya, Kafr al Shaikh, Giza, and Fayoum. In one governorate, Sohag, the capital city has the same number of both governmental and private mosques. And in the following seven governorates, the districts have more governmental mosques than do the capital cities: Gharbiya, Qalyubiya, Sharqiya, Daqhaliya, Damietta, Minya, and Aswan. Although these seven districts have more governmental mosques than do the capital cities and a lower density of population, nevertheless all but one of them (Aswan) still have more male Muslims per mosque. Put another way, the urban concentration of governmental mosques is seen in the fact that although the capital cities are more densely populated, the six of them which have fewer mosques than their districts also have fewer male Muslims per mosque. This means that the district's larger number of mosques is usually not enough to compensate for its larger population.

For private mosques, the distribution is somewhat different. In eleven governorates (all but Giza and Qalyubiya) the district has more mosques than the capital city, whereas in the case of governmental mosques only seven districts have more mosques than their capital cities do. The survey does not give the number of male Muslims per private mosque, but since this type is the far more numerous one, it determines the number of male Muslims for each of both types, which we have just reviewed. We may safely say, then, that the distribution of private mosques is the more 'normal' in the sense that the capital city has fewer private mosques and a higher density of population and, as a result, also has more male Muslims per mosque.

Population per mosque is more meaningful when considered in relation to the size of mosques themselves. Obviously, the larger mosques in major cities can easily accommodate more people than the smaller mosques. Table 2 roughly suggests the size of mosques in the various governorates. Though this table is useful, it has two serious limitations. First, its categories—excellent, large, medium and small—are not measures along a single scale. 'Excellent' (mumtāz) seems to include a qualitative judgement as well as the quantitative one implied in the other three terms: kabīr, mutawassiṭ, and ṣaghīr. The term is not explained in the survey, but it seems to refer to a mosque of at least moderate size, with excellent facilities, and maintained in superior condition. A mosque judged to be 'mumtāz', therefore, need not be the largest despite the fact that this category precedes all the others in the table. On the other hand, 'mumtāz' may simply mean a monumental or extra-large mosque. Second, the survey does not indicate the criteria used in deciding how to place each mosque. Since the survey was made by local officials, it is likely that judgments as to what is excellent, large, medium and small varied according to the observer from region to region and even within the same region. Thus the Fayoum has twenty-four 'excellent' governmental mosques and Cairo only eight more. Also, 42 per cent of the governmental mosques in Alexandria are classified as 'small' but only 20 per cent of those in Buhaira. If all the judgments

TABLE 2. *Size of governmental and private mosques, 1962, by governorate*

Governorate and type	Excellent[a]		Large		Medium		Small		Not reported		Total	
	No.	%	No.	%	No.	%	No.	%	No.	%	No.	%
Cairo												
Governmental	32	6	77	15	186	36	195	37	33	6	523	100
Private	9	4	23	10	106	49	43	20	37	17	218	100
Alexandria												
Governmental	5	3	20	12	61	37	69	42	10	6	165	100
Private	3	2	35	20	55	32	72	42	7	4	172	100
Port Said												
Governmental	7	54	1	8	3	23	2	15	—	—	13	100
Private	1	4	2	7	24	89	—	—	—	—	27	100
Ismailiya												
Governmental	4	29	3	21	4	29	3	21	—	—	14	100
Private	1	1	29	13	52	24	133	61	3	1	218	100
Suez												
Governmental	—	—	4	36	5	46	1	9	1	9	11	100
Private	4	7	4	7	13	22	37	61	2	3	60	100
Damietta												
Governmental	7	9	19	25	42	54	9	12	—	—	77	100
Private	3	3	17	20	34	40	32	37	—	—	86	100

Daqhaliya												
Governmental	20	7	63	22	125	43	62	22	17	6	287	100
Private	25	2	151	12	249	20	152	13	640	53	1,217	100
Sharqiya												
Governmental	10	6	53	32	48	29	13	8	42	25	166	100
Private	141	8	299	17	750	42	104	6	493	27	1,787	100
Qalyubiya												
Governmental	12	10	57	50	34	30	10	9	1	1	114	100
Private	24	5	113	23	202	42	123	26	20	4	482	100
Kafr al Shaikh												
Governmental	15	10	72	50	41	28	15	10	2	2	145	100
Private	26	4	131	21	315	50	109	17	51	8	632	100
Gharbiya												
Governmental	10	4	56	20	128	46	29	11	52	19	275	100
Private	27	4	151	20	383	50	120	16	78	10	759	100
Minoufiya												
Governmental	3	2	12	8	50	36	67	48	8	6	140	100
Private	4	4	55	6	293	32	547	60	16	2	915	100
Buhaira												
Governmental	12	6	61	31	77	40	39	20	5	3	194	100
Private	16	2	119	14	408	49	265	32	27	3	835	100
Giza												
Governmental	1	1	14	18	12	16	1	1	49	64	77	100
Private	37	8	123	27	182	40	49	11	66	14	457	100

TABLE 2 (cont.)

Governorate and type	Excellent[a]		Large		Medium		Small		Not reported		Total	
	No.	%	No.	%	No.	%	No.	%	No.	%	No.	%
Beni Suef												
Governmental	16	12	41	31	62	47	10	8	3	2	132	100
Private	44	10	81	19	213	50	68	16	19	5	425	100
Fayoum												
Governmental	24	32	17	23	20	26	8	11	6	8	75	100
Private	31	5	118	21	241	42	126	22	59	10	575	100
Minya												
Governmental	17	9	62	35	83	47	9	5	8	4	179	100
Private	23	3	146	17	599	69	90	10	13	1	871	100
Assiut												
Governmental	9	7	28	23	52	42	21	17	13	11	123	100
Private	39	5	101	13	386	49	215	28	41	5	782	100
Sohag												
Governmental	13	12	24	22	41	37	27	25	5	4	110	100
Private	46	2	201	10	791	40	727	37	218	11	1,983	100
Qena												
Governmental	—	—	—	—	—	—	—	—	101	—	101	100
Private	100	7	215	16	384	28	177	13	494	36	1,370	100

24

Aswan												
Governmental	11	21	12	23	21	40	5	10	3	6	52	100
Private	2	1	18	7	118	47	111	44	2	1	251	100
Red Sea												
Governmental	—	—	1	12	2	25	3	38	2	25	8	100
Private	—	—	—	—	2	33	4	67	—	—	6	100
Southern Desert												
Governmental	—	—	—	—	—	—	—	—	—	—	—	—
Private	—	—	—	—	29	97	1	3	—	—	30	100
Western Desert												
Governmental	—	—	—	—	—	—	—	—	—	—	—	—
Private	—	—	—	—	—	—	—	—	37	100	37	100
Sinai												
Governmental	3	19	3	19	3	19	7	43	—	—	16	100
Private	—	—	1	6	6	35	10	59	—	—	17	100
Total												
Governmental	231	8	700	23	1,100	37	605	20	361	12	2,997	100
Private	606	4	2,133	15	5,835	41	3,315	23	2,323	17	14,212	100
All mosques	837	5	2,833	16	6,935	40	3,920	23	2,684	16	17,209	100

ᵃ mumtāz.

Sources: Governmental mosques—Ministry of Waqfs 1963, table, p. 137.
Private mosques—Ministry of Waqfs 1964a, table, p. 41.

had been made upon clear, objective criteria or subjectively by the same observer accustomed, let us say, to the scale of mosques in Cairo, the results would undoubtedly have been very different.

Table 2 does, nevertheless, enable us to make some reliable observations and comparisons. Of all 17,209 mosques classified, 5 per cent are classified as excellent and another 16 per cent as large. Since by far the larger proportion of mosques are private, it is their size that determines the distribution of the total number. Governmental mosques, then, have higher proportions—8 and 23 per cent respectively—in these two categories of the better and more important mosques. Within most of the governorates the same relationship obtains: the governmental mosques are more likely to be the ones regarded as excellent and largest. There is, however, an important distinction here. In almost all regions the governmental mosques regarded as large are more numerous than the private ones in that category, even though the total number of private mosques is greater in all regions except Cairo and the Red Sea. In addition, the governmental mosques regarded as excellent are also the more numerous in the large urban regions such as Cairo, Alexandria and Port Said. In the provincial places, however, most of the excellent mosques one is likely to see are private ones. Thus in Damietta, Daqhaliya, Sharqiya, and so on, the actual number of private mosques that are excellent is greater than that of the governmental ones, though the latter have a higher proportion rated excellent. It should be noted, also, that only 986 of the 14,212 private mosques, or 7 per cent, receive a subsidy from the government.[1] The amount of this assistance is not specified.

The impressive number and condition of so many private mosques in the provincial cities of secondary rank is probably the result of waqfs established by that class of large land-

[1] Ministry of Waqfs 1964*a*, p. 39.

holders (and their descendants) which was itself created in the late nineteenth and early twentieth centuries.[1] Although the surveys contain information about the age of the mosques, they do not present the kind of data that would enable us to trace the age of mosques in relation to their size and location.

Table 3 summarizes the data on the age of mosques. Of nearly 17,000 governmental and private mosques, there is no information on about 2,500, or 15 per cent. The remaining 14,500 are nearly equally distributed among three age groups. Almost 5,000, or about 30 per cent, are less than thirty years old. A like number are between thirty and sixty-nine years old. The remaining 4,500 are seventy years and older; this group includes 176 governmental mosques classed as antiquities, 140 of which are in Cairo. The governmental mosques are older (even excluding the 176 classed as antiquities) than the private ones. Only 21 per cent of the governmental mosques are in the youngest category, compared with 30 per cent of the private mosques; but 39 per cent of the governmental mosques are in the oldest category, compared with only 24 per cent of the private mosques.

Among the governmental mosques themselves, there is some regional variation with respect to age. Of the urban governorates, the older cities of Cairo and Alexandria have of course a greater concentration of older mosques than do the younger ones like Ismailiya and Suez. The Lower Egypt provinces have a higher proportion of mosques in the oldest group than do the provinces of Upper Egypt, where the middle category has the highest proportion. As for the private mosques, in most governorates, with some scattered exceptions, they are concentrated in the younger age groups.

Maintenance of buildings in Egypt is notoriously poor, and the maintenance of mosques is probably on about the same level, judging from the low proportion of nineteenth-

[1] Baer 1962, Chapter II.

TABLE 3. *Age of governmental and private mosques in 1962, by governorate*

Governorate and type	Under 30 years		30–69 years		70 years and over[a]		Not reported		Total[b]	
	No.	%	No.	%	No.	%	No.	%	No.	%
Cairo										
Governmental	49	10	103	21	302	62	33	7	487	100
Private	105	48	55	25	21	10	37	17	218	100
Alexandria										
Governmental	26	18	64	45	51	36	1	1	142	100
Private	89	52	64	37	10	6	9	5	172	100
Port Said										
Governmental	1	25	—	—	—	—	3	75	4	100
Private	14	52	12	44	—	—	1	2	27	100
Ismailiya										
Governmental	8	47	5	29	2	12	2	12	17	100
Private	135	62	75	34	4	2	4	2	218	100
Suez										
Governmental	6	55	2	18	3	27	—	—	11	100
Private	46	76	10	17	1	2	3	5	60	100
Damietta										
Governmental	33	43	6	8	37	49	—	—	76	100
Private	60	70	19	22	5	6	2	2	86	100

	1	2	3	4	5	6	7	8	9	10
Daqhaliya										
Governmental	60	24	73	29	100	40	19	7	252	100
Private	369	30	174	14	56	5	618	51	1,217	100
Sharqiya										
Governmental	34	23	23	16	26	18	63	43	146	100
Private	517	29	468	26	256	14	546	31	1,787	100
Qalyubiya										
Governmental	29	26	33	30	36	33	12	11	110	100
Private	173	36	140	29	138	29	31	6	482	100
Kafr al Shaikh										
Governmental	33	21	42	27	70	44	12	8	157	100
Private	328	52	176	28	66	10	62	10	632	100
Gharbiya										
Governmental	46	17	55	20	145	53	27	10	273	100
Private	227	30	309	41	202	26	21	3	759	100
Minoufiya										
Governmental	38	27	56	40	32	23	15	10	141	100
Private	252	28	194	21	448	49	21	2	915	100
Buhaira										
Governmental	52	26	73	35	73	35	8	4	206	100
Private	418	50	259	31	115	14	43	5	835	100
Giza										
Governmental	17	28	22	36	18	29	4	7	61	100
Private	151	33	135	30	133	30	38	8	457	100

TABLE 3 (continued)

Governorate and type	Under 30 years		30–69 years		70 years and over[a]		Not reported		Total[b]	
	No.	%	No.	%	No.	%	No.	%	No.	%
Beni Suef										
Governmental	28	21	57	43	45	34	2	2	132	100
Private	149	35	181	43	83	19	12	3	425	100
Fayoum										
Governmental	19	25	44	59	9	12	3	4	75	100
Private	153	27	172	30	64	11	186	32	575	100
Minya										
Governmental	25	14	111	62	33	18	10	6	179	100
Private	122	14	568	65	136	16	45	5	871	100
Assiut										
Governmental	22	18	28	23	44	36	29	23	123	100
Private	225	29	271	35	263	33	23	3	782	100
Sohag										
Governmental	31	28	45	41	32	29	2	2	110	100
Private	437	22	575	29	897	45	74	4	1,983	100
Qena										
Governmental[c]	163	12	256	19	444	32	507	37	1,370	100
Aswan										
Governmental	29	56	11	22	12	22	—	—	52	100
Private	105	42	77	31	59	23	10	4	251	100

Red Sea										
Governmental	4	57	1	14	2	29	—	—	7	100
Private	4	66	1	17	1	17	—	—	6	100
Southern Desert										
Governmental[c]										
Private	10	33	19	64	—	1		3	30	100
Western Desert										
Governmental	3	50	2	33	1	17	—	—	6	100
Private							37	100	37	100
Sinai										
Governmental	3	60	1	20	1	20	—	—	5	100
Private	14	82	2	12	1	6	—	—	17	100
Total										
Governmental	596	21	857	31	1,074	39	245	9	2,772	100
Private	4,266	30	4,212	30	3,403	24	2,331	16	14,212	100
All mosques	4,862	29	5,069	30	4,477	26	2,576	15	16,984	100

[a] Includes 176 governmental mosques so old as to be classed as antiquities :
Cairo 140, Alexandria 1, Buhaira 1, Gharbiya 13, Qalyubiya 6, Fayoum 1, Beni Suef 1, Damietta 1, Minya 3, Assiut 8, Sohag 1.

[b] The totals for governmental mosques given in this source differ slightly from those given in the source for Table 1.

[c] No figures given.

Sources: Governmental mosques—Ministry of Waqfs 1963, p. 109.
Private mosques—Ministry of Waqfs 1964a, p. 42.

century mosques surviving in 1962. Of 14,408 governmental and private mosques whose age is given in table 3, less than a third were seventy or more years old.

The two surveys give much direct information on the state of repair of the mosques and the facilities they afford worshippers.

Table 4 summarizes one aspect of this subject, the number of mosques which could and could not be used at all for religious services. Only 192 of nearly 17,000 mosques were in so bad a state that they were not actually in use. Table 5, however, gives another indication of physical condition. Of nearly 17,000 mosques, 71 per cent are in good condition, 10 per cent need repairs which if completed would make these mosques fully sound, 3 per cent are only partly reparable, and another 3 per cent are not at all reparable; on the remaining 13 per cent there was no information. If we omit the mosques whose condition is not reported, then the private mosques are in a somewhat better state of repair than the table suggests, and the differences between the two kinds become almost negligible.

Table 4 shows that 192 mosques are in such bad condition ('in ruins') that no religious services are performed in them. Table 5, however, lists 375 mosques as totally irreparable and 'crumbling'. This difference indicates that there must be nearly two hundred mosques, mostly private, in which religious services are performed even though their condition is described as 'crumbling'.

The surveys give data on the number and condition of public conveniences in the mosques. Table 6 shows the number of such facilities. This kind of wholesale reporting, however, is of limited use. We can see that 16,601 mosques have about 115,000 water faucets but we cannot determine the number of mosques that have and that lack each kind of convenience. For the private mosques alone this information is summarized in table 7. It shows that ablution taps and W.C.s, the facilities most urgently required by religious injunction, are also those most generally available; yet more than a quarter of the private mosques lack them. The two other conveniences, baths and urinals, are less urgent needs and are indeed lacking in most private mosques. From table 6 we may deduce that the availability of sanitary facilities is probably not much different in the governmental mosques; the ratio of ablution taps to mosques is nearly twelve to one, whereas baths and urinals both are fewer than the number of mosques. Further light is thrown on this point in table 8, which also summarizes the survey's evaluation of the condition and sufficiency of public conveniences in both governmental and private mosques. Of the nearly 17,000 mosques, over 1,100, or 7 per cent, are entirely lacking in public conveniences, and another 2,356, or 14 per cent, do not have enough. Fewer than half of all the mosques are said to have an adequate number of conveniences in good condition. The governmental mosques make somewhat better provision in this respect than do the private ones, many of which are small and not maintained regularly.

The survey of private mosques reports on three other facilities (for which there are no corresponding data for governmental mosques): electricity, microphones and libraries. Table 9 shows that very few private mosques have any of them; a higher proportion of governmental mosques probably do. The government has encouraged the establishment of libraries as a means of widening the mosque's role as a cultural and educational center. As we saw earlier, it has established a new mosque post, mosque attendant (muqīm al-shaʿāʾir), one of whose explicit duties is to run the mosque library. The use of the microphone for the call to prayer seems to visitors to have increased greatly in recent years. This may be so, yet only 440 of the more than 14,000 private mosques

TABLE 4. *Use of mosques for religious services*

Type of mosque	In use		Not in use[a]		Not reported		Total	
	No.	%	No.	%	No.	%	No.	%
Governmental	2,561	93	95	3	116	4	2,772	100
Private	12,090	85	97	1	2,025	14	14,212	100
All mosques	14,651	86	192	1	2,141	13	16,984	100

[a] Mukharrab or mukhrab, literally: in ruins.

Sources: Governmental mosques—Ministry of Waqfs 1963, p. 101.
Private mosques—Ministry of Waqfs 1964*a*, p. 40.

TABLE 5. *State of repair of mosques*

Type of mosque	Good		Fully reparable		Partly reparable		Totally irreparable		Not reported		Total	
	No.	%	No.	%	No.	%	No.	%	No.	%	No.	%
Governmental	2,050	74	332	12	88	3	155	6	147	5	2,772	100
Private	10,140	71	1,341	9	433	3	220	2	2,078	15	14,212	100
All mosques	12,190	71	1,673	10	521	3	375	3	2,225	13	16,984	100

Sources: Governmental mosques—Ministry of Waqfs 1963, p. 102.
Private mosques—Ministry of Waqfs 1964*a*, p. 43.

TABLE 6. *Number of public conveniences in mosques*

Type of mosque	No. of mosques	No. of ablution taps	No. of baths	No. of urinals	No. of w.c.s
Governmental	2,389	28,501	1,331	864	12,739
Private	14,212	86,497	8,609	1,188	44,834
All mosques	16,601	114,998	9,940	2,052	57,573

Sources: Governmental mosques—Ministry of Waqfs 1963, p. 103.
Private mosques—Ministry of Waqfs 1964a, p. 52.

TABLE 7. *Public conveniences in private mosques*

	Ablution taps		Baths		Urinals		W.C.s	
	No. of mosques	%	No. of mosques	%	No. of mosques	%	No. of mosques	%
Present	10,286	72	6,507	46	773	5	10,274	72
Absent	3,926	28	7,705	54	13,439	95	3,938	28
Total	14,212	100	14,212	100	14,212	100	14,212	100

Source: Ministry of Waqfs 1964a, pp. 53–6.

3-2

TABLE 8. *Adequacy*[a] *of public conveniences in mosques*

Type of mosque	Good and sufficient		Good but not sufficient		Not good		Not present		Not reported		Total	
	No.	%	No.	%	No.	%	No.	%	No.	%	No.	%
Governmental	1,458	53	450	16	396	14	126	5	342	12	2,772	100
Private	6,281	44	1,906	14	1,592	11	994	7	3,439	24	14,212	100
All mosques	7,739	45	2,356	14	1,988	12	1,120	7	3,781	22	16,984	100

[a] 'Good' refers to condition of the conveniences; 'sufficient' refers to their number in relation to need.

Sources: Governmental mosques—Ministry of Waqfs 1963, p. 104.
Private mosques—Ministry of Waqfs 1964a, p. 57.

TABLE 9. *Electricity, microphones, and libraries in private mosques*

	Electricity		Microphones		Library	
	No. of mosques	%	No. of mosques	%	No. of mosques	%
Present	1,332	9	440	3	326	2
Absent	9,329	66	8,752	62	10,775	76
Not reported	3,551	25	5,020	35	3,111	22
Total	14,212	100	14,212	100	14,212	100

Source: Ministry of Waqfs 1964*a*, compiled from tables on pp. 65–7.

in the entire country specifically indicate having one. Of those that have a loud speaker system, 150 use it to announce all five daily prayers and 190 use it only for the Friday noon prayer. Hearing only one amplified call to prayer, however, may easily lead one to assume there are many. In Cairo, for example, eighteen private mosques were reported as using the microphone for all five daily prayers; hearing one of these calls would obscure the fact that sixty-six more private mosques in Cairo were not using their microphones at all except for the Friday noon prayer.

The surveys present a large amount of information about mosque officials and servants: their number, educational background, and compensation. Only a small portion of this information is appropriate here.

Table 10 shows that in 1962 there were about 53,500 people employed in all mosques. Imams and muezzins, each with about 14,000, together accounted for about half of the total, reciters of the Koran for a tenth, and servants for about two fifths. Private mosques had about four fifths of all officials and employees, which is about the same proportion of these mosques to the total number. Since private mosques employ

TABLE 10. *Mosque personnel, 1962*

Type of mosque	Imams		Muezzins		Koran reciters		Servants		Total	
	No.	%	No.	%	No.	%	No.	%	No.	%
Governmental	2,147	21	2,091	21	1,376	14	4,459	44	10,073	100
Private	12,283	28	11,262	26	3,242	8	16,682	38	43,469	100
All mosques	14,430	27	13,353	25	4,618	9	21,141	39	53,542	100

Source: Ministry of Waqfs 1964 *a*, p. 6.

TABLE 11. *Pay status of private mosque personnel*

Post	Paid officials		Unpaid volunteers		Total	
	No.	%	No.	%	No.	%
Imams	2,086	17	10,197	83	12,283	100
Muezzins	1,680	15	9,582	85	11,262	100
Reciters	535	17	2,707	83	3,242	100
Servants	2,731	16	13,951	84	16,682	100
Total	7,032	16	36,437	84	43,469	100

Source: Ministry of Waqfs 1964*a*, p. 7.

so large a proportion of all mosque personnel, their distribution determines the distribution of all mosque personnel. The pattern of employment in governmental mosques is, however, somewhat different. In them imams and muezzins each account only for about a fifth of all personnel, which is less than the corresponding proportion in private mosques. Koran reciters in governmental mosques are 14 per cent of all personnel in these mosques, as against only 8 per cent in the private mosques. Servants, also, comprise a higher proportion of governmental than of private mosque personnel. The distribution of personnel per mosque, at least for imams and muezzins, comes to what one would expect: roughly one of each per mosque, whether governmental or private. Koran reciters are much rarer; fewer than half of the governmental mosques and only about a quarter of the private ones have a specially designated and trained reciter. The distribution of servants is probably more uneven. There is an average of only 1·5 servants per governmental mosque; and since many have two or more, it follows that many have no regularly employed servants. Private mosques are not so well off as this, having a slightly lower ratio of servants to mosques (1·2 to 1).

The employment status of mosque officials differs. In the governmental mosques, most of the higher officials are civil servants, in the private mosques none of them are. Even among the imams, the highest mosque officials, not all are civil servants even in governmental mosques. Of 2,147 imams in governmental mosques, 921, or 43 per cent, receive compensation called mukāfāt,[1] which means a regular salary but not a regular or permanent post with pension rights and the usual perquisites of a civil service appointment.

---

[1] According to Ministry of Waqfs 1963, first table on p.10. If one calculates the number of these imams on non-tenure appointments from other figures, the result is slightly different: 980 out of 2,123, or 47 per cent (*ibid.* tables 2–5 pp. 6–8).

Generally, persons in this category have less training for the post and receive less pay in it than do those who hold similar posts in the regular table of organization.

In the private mosques, all officials and servants either receive compensation called mukāfāt, and hence have no regular tenure, or they are volunteers who are not paid at all. Table 11 shows that the vast majority in all four posts are unpaid volunteers; only a sixth are paid. This means that the religious life of the people is still a largely voluntary and spontaneous activity, for 83 per cent of all mosques are privately supported and 84 per cent of all officials in these private mosques are unpaid volunteers. They are also not highly trained, a fact that has disturbed the governmental authorities; efforts have been made to increase the formal training of mosque officials and, we have already seen, the government has taken over hundreds of private mosques under a law of 1960.

The lower qualifications of officials in private mosques is clearly shown in tables 12, 13, and 14. Table 12 shows that more than half of the imams in governmental mosques have higher education, compared with a negligible 2 per cent in private mosques. At the other end, the imams with no educational qualifications at all comprise four fifths of all imams in private mosques but only one fifth of all those in governmental mosques. Even the government imams on non-tenure appointment are better qualified than the imams in private mosques; of these governmental imams, about a fifth have higher degrees or diplomas.[1]

The difference in educational background is not so marked for muezzins, but those employed in governmental mosques are better qualified. Over a tenth of the governmental muezzins have at least some educational qualifications, compared with fewer than 2 per cent of those in private mosques, as Table 13 shows.

[1] Ministry of Waqfs 1963, first table on p. 10.

TABLE 12. *Educational qualifications of imams*

Type of mosque	High[a]		Intermediate[b]		Below intermediate		None		Total	
	No.	%	No.	%	No.	%	No.	%	No.	%
Governmental	1,108	52	367	17	226	10	446	21	2,147	100
Private	227	2	716	6	1,630	13	9,710	79	12,283	100
All mosques	1,335	9	1,083	8	1,856	13	10,156	70	14,430	100

[a] University degree or diploma from an institute beyond secondary school.
[b] Secondary school certificate.

Sources: Governmental mosques—Ministry of Waqfs 1963, p. 6, table 1.
Private mosques—Ministry of Waqfs 1964a, p. 9.

TABLE 13. *Educational qualifications of muezzins*

Type of mosque	High		Intermediate		Below intermediate		None		Total	
	No.	%	No.	%	No.	%	No.	%	No.	%
Governmental	14	0·6	45	2	171	8	1,993	90	2,223	100
Private	—	—	21	0·2	173	1·5	11,068	98	11,262	100
All mosques	14	0·1	66	0·5	344	2·5	13,061	97	13,485	100

Note: see footnotes to Table 12.
Sources: Governmental mosques—Ministry of Waqfs 1963, p. 42.
Private mosques—Ministry of Waqfs 1964a, p. 15.

TABLE 14. *Educational qualifications of Koran reciters*

Type of mosque	High		Intermediate		Below intermediate		None		Total	
	No.	%	No.	%	No.	%	No.	%	No.	%
Governmental	10	0·7	12	0·8	81	6	1,273	93	1,376	100
Private	4	0·1	7	0·2	76	2	3,155	97	3,242	100
All mosques	14	0·3	19	0·4	157	3	4,428	96	4,618	100

Note: See footnotes to table 12.
Sources: Governmental mosques—Ministry of Waqfs 1963, p. 58.
Private mosques—Ministry of Waqfs 1964a, p. 21.

TABLE 15. *Monthly salaries of imams without permanent status in governmental and private mosques, 1962*
(in Egyptian pounds)

Type of mosque	Less than 2		2–4		5–6		7 and more		Total	
	No.	%	No.	%	No.	%	No.	%	No.	%
Governmental	43	5	396	47	214	25	188	23	841	100
Private	1,298	62	579	28	88	4	121	6	2,086	100
All mosques	1,341	46	975	33	302	10	309	11	2,927	100

Sources: Governmental mosques—Ministry of Waqfs 1963, adapted from tables on pp. 10–11.
Private mosques—Ministry of Waqfs 1964a, adapted from table on p. 11.

Religious organization

As for Koran reciters, table 14 shows a smaller gap. In governmental mosques, 6 per cent have some qualifications, as compared with only 2 per cent in private mosques.

No strict comparison of salaries in governmental and private mosques is possible because of the disparity in training and education of the officials of each type, and the civil service status of a large proportion of the imams in governmental mosques. As we saw earlier, imams in that status receive monthly salaries ranging from twenty to ninety Egyptian pounds, according to rank. Others, in non-permanent posts, receive much lower pay. The imams in private mosques are mainly unpaid volunteers, but those who are paid at all receive less than even non-permanent imams in governmental mosques, as table 15 shows. The survey provides information on 841 of the more than 900 imams without permanent status in governmental mosques. Of them, nearly three quarters were paid between two and seven pounds monthly in 1962, a rather moderate income even for Egypt. But the imams in private mosques were paid even less; three fifths received under two pounds monthly. The gap is similar for muezzins, but for Koran reciters the gap almost disappears.[1]

A more recent official report than the two surveys we have been using indicates that the number of officials and employees in governmental mosques has grown considerably since 1951. Table 16 gives this comparison as of 1963, when the number of officials was greater than that reported by the survey as of 1962. (See table 10 above.) For all posts, the increase was about four fifths. The number of imams more than doubled, muezzins rose by about three quarters, and reciters and servants by about two thirds.

[1] On muezzins and reciters in governmental mosques: Ministry of Waqfs 1963, pp. 43, 59. On muezzins and reciters in private mosques: Ministry of Waqfs 1964a, pp. 17, 23.

TABLE 16. *Increase in governmental mosque personnel, 1951–1963*

Post	1951	1963	Increase 1951–63	
			No.	%
Imams	1,552	3,257	1,705	109
Muezzins	1,437	2,550	1,113	77
Reciters	960	1,650	690	68
Servants[a]	2,970	4,900	1,930	65
Total	6,919	12,357	5,438	79

[a] Including overseers of servants.

Source: Ministry of Waqfs 1964*b*, p. 79.

RECENT GOVERNMENTAL POLICY TOWARD RELIGIOUS INSTITUTIONS

For a long time Egyptian rulers have been increasing their power over religious institutions by tightening their control over the religious leaders and transferring their functions, especially in education and justice, to the secular authorities.[1] This tendency, accelerated by the military leaders who overthrew the monarchy in 1952, has not been aimed merely at aggrandizing state power at the expense of the power that religious loyalty and religious leaders exerted over the Muslim population. Long before 1952 various governments in Egypt had sought to eliminate certain popular religious practices, such as saint-worship, animism, and exhibitionism, which were regarded by the authorities as weaknesses, abuses or worse. Governmental regulation of virtually all aspects of social life was growing; it was, therefore, not surprising that religious institutions should also be the object of reform by the secular power. Since 1952, however, the state has pursued a much more coordinated and intensive policy, with ideological overtones indicating that the reform or elevation of reli-

[1] On this process in the nineteenth century in the Ottoman Empire, see the article by Bernard Lewis on Bāb-i Mashīkhat, in *E.I.*[2].

gious practice has been secondary to the goal of increasing state power over public attitudes and behavior. This new balance of goals became clear fairly early in the regime's career, when it completed the process by which Al-Azhar became completely dependent upon the government financially and in general policy, and decided, in 1955, to abolish rather than merely to reform the religious (shar'ī) courts. The road to reform, it became clear, would lead not merely to the end of recognized abuses but also to unchallenged state control and the consequent weakening of religious leadership (which though generally subservient had at least retained some basis for potential independence), and to a reduction of the autonomy of popular religious institutions.

The military regime's self-confidence in seeking to transform religious institutions stands in marked contrast to the timidity of those other innovators, the colonial powers. In 1891 Lord Cromer reported abuses in the shar'ī courts and the administration of waqfs but he warned that on these subjects 'the interference of any European, or, indeed, of any Christian, is undesirable and impossible'.[1] The recent transformation has already encompassed the courts; its other center of action has been the functions of the Ministry of Waqfs, which not only administered these pious foundations but had since the late nineteenth century been performing an increasing number of other religious functions. With secularization, the Ministry became a target of reformers for two reasons: the institution of the waqf itself came under attack, and the abuses (perhaps inevitable where great wealth is concerned) in their handling by the Ministry likewise aroused criticism. The Sanitation Committee for Mosque Improvement in 1942 drew attention to the reduction in the powers of the Ministry in the previous two decades. Schools which

[1] *Report on the Administration and Condition of Egypt and the Progress of Reforms*, 29 March 1891. Egypt. No. 3 (1891), pp. 23–4.

it once supervised were transferred to the Ministry of Education. Financial support of Al-Azhar and its several institutes had been shifted from the Ministry of Waqfs to the general treasury. Other activities of the Ministry had declined considerably, and the committee expected these to be distributed among other ministries, in accordance with the established trend. Mosque administration was the only function of the Ministry that had grown; indeed, the Committee anticipated, approvingly, that this function would soon be the Ministry's only one.[1]

Transfer of functions and powers from the Ministry of Waqfs to other governmental agencies thus preceded the advent of the military regime in 1952, but that regime stepped up the process. Soon after it assumed power, the regime introduced land reform and abolished all waqfs for private (family) purposes; the land held under these waqfs was made available for distribution under the land reform. It next transferred to the Ministry of Waqfs the management of all charitable waqfs (for public purposes). At first these reforms seem to have increased the functions and powers of the Ministry of Waqfs; but this was not the case, because the land under family waqfs was transferred to and then distributed by the Ministry of Agrarian Reform, while the mere prospect of the Ministry's ultimate management of all other waqfs simply meant that not many such bequests would be made any more.[2]

Very soon after coming to power, the military regime sought new instruments for two purposes regarding Islam in Egypt: first, to mobilize the masses for the new internal goals and to neutralize the potential opposition or indifference to them on the part of the religious masses and leaders; second, to use Islam in the furtherance of the regime's foreign policy

[1] Sanitation Committee, pp. 1, 2.
[2] Ministry of Waqfs 1964*b*, pp. 35–8.

in the Arab world and Africa. This policy was strengthened as the regime seemed to recognize more and more that Islam remained the widest and most effective basis for consensus despite all efforts to promote nationalism, patriotism, secularism, and socialism.

The Islamic Congress (al-mu'tamar al-Islāmī), an international organization with headquarters in Cairo, was the first instrument available to the new regime. Egyptian officials loyal to the military regime controlled the Congress but its international character placed some limits upon their power to bend it to the regime's purpose. That purpose, however, was not concealed, for the Congress was supported generously while Al-Azhar, for example, was being further restricted and then in 1961 vastly transformed. In 1958 I interviewed the head of the Congress, an Army officer who was a member of the Revolutionary Command Council, the group of twelve military men who led the overthrow of the monarchy in 1952. I asked him if the Congress was intended by the regime to replace all existing agencies as the religious guide for the masses of Egyptians. He replied that it was, explaining that traditional agencies were unable to adjust to the new needs of the Islamic community in the modern world.

In the Ministry of Waqfs, meanwhile, the Directorate General for the propagation of Islam (al-idāra al-'āmma li-l da'wa al-Islāmīya) continued to perform its similar functions. In 1960, however, the military regime established within the Ministry the Supreme Council for Islamic Affairs (al-majlis al-a'lā li-l shu'ūn al-Islāmīya), an agency that has become virtually an autonomous parallel to the Ministry itself. The identity of function appears in an official description of the two agencies. The Directorate General in the Ministry is said to be charged with (1) the 'diffusion of Islamic culture and the arousal of religious consciousness in the whole Arab nation in order to make Islam known among all peoples of the world,' (2) the 'preservation of the Koran by its publication, and the execution of its printing and distribution,' and (3) supervision of the affairs of mosques so that they may properly fulfill their mission in the spreading of Islam and in strengthening the spiritual and moral character of Arab society. The Council, in the same official document, is said to be charged with exactly the same duty, in exactly the same language describing the first of the Directorate General's functions.[1] What, then, is the difference between the work of the two agencies? The document goes on to list the special powers of the Council, but these do not distinguish it from the Directorate General, whose special functions of translation, publication, education, and so on, are quite similar.

The difference appears in the general statement about the Council: 'This eminent Islamic body was established in 1960 to fulfill its religious mission on a large scale and over a broad area, and to extend its brilliant rays of light from the United Arab Republic to all quarters of the world, East and West equally, regardless of race and color... The noble objective of the Supreme Council of Islamic Affairs requires that it be completely free of the restraints of routine, so that it may proceed to its goal free of all shackles... '[2] Thus the Council, as contrasted with the Directorate General it parallels (or displaces?) is described as 'eminent', having an especially broad mission that stresses its source in the U.A.R. particularly (rather than in Islam or the Arab nation), and as requiring freedom from bureaucratic routine. Though the Council was placed in the Ministry of Waqfs and the Minister was made its head, the Council's special status was signalized by appointment of a secretary-general to administer

[1] Ministry of Waqfs 1964*b*, pp. 45, 117.
[2] Ministry of Waqfs 1964*b*, p. 115.

it.[1] Since its creation, the Council has become increasingly autonomous in policy and budget.

True to its charter, the Council has pursued an independent course under the direction of a young army officer as its secretary-general. The Council has regarded the Ministry of Waqfs as reactionary and incapable of meeting the modern challenge, while the older religious establishment has regarded the Council as a political tool of the regime that ultimately brings harm to Islam, and as 'modern' ('aṣrī) or libertine, a meaning of this word common in Egypt until about a quarter-century ago. The Council has commissioned many booklets on various aspects of Islam and has provided scholarships, services, and activities for many young men, from other Islamic countries, studying in Egypt. It has also sponsored visits of scholars and leading personalities from abroad, including the American Muhammad Ali (Cassius Clay).[2] Finally, it has distributed books and journals on Islamic subjects to many countries. Table 17 presents an interesting sidelight on this activity. Although Egypt has for years maintained better diplomatic relations with the Soviet Union than with the United States, and although the Soviet Union has millions of Muslims and the United States proably no more than a hundred thousand, the Council has sent far more literature to the United States than to the Soviet Union.

Erosion of the functions and powers of the Ministry of Waqfs has left it with three main areas: charity, investments of its own funds, and mosque supervision.

The Ministry makes charity donations to individuals and organizations. In 1963–4, most of the individual cases were the aged and widows; also included were the sick, divorcées and spinsters, wives of prisoners, unemployed, and students.

---

[1] Ministry of Waqfs 1964*b*, pp. 118, 121.
[2] Ministry of Waqfs 1964*b*, p. 53.

TABLE 17. *Number of books and journals sent to the U.S.S.R. and the U.S.A. by the Supreme Council of Islamic Affairs, 1960–1964*

	U.S.S.R.	U.S.A.
1960	—	700
1961	—	2,333
1962[a]		
1963	—	1,243
1964	190	1,144

[a] Not mentioned.

Source: Ministry of Waqfs 1964*b*, pp. 134, 137.

The total spent for these and other charities was £E 329,500 in 1952–3; though this budget later rose somewhat, in 1963–4 it was at almost the same level, £E 340,000.[1] During this period prices and population rose but this was probably offset by increases in payments under old and new governmental welfare schemes run by other ministries. The Ministry has also had a small program of interest-free loans to Muslims; these loans do not exceed twenty-five Egyptian pounds, are repayable in one year, and are for amounts up to 60 per cent of the articles put up for security. The amount spent on such loans has risen steadily from nearly £E 26,000 in 1952–3 to almost £E 80,000 in 1963–4. This program was designed, of course, to help poor people avoid pawnbrokers and usurers.[2]

A very important, though increasingly circumscribed, power of the Ministry of Waqfs has been that of investing its surplus funds originating in waqfs under its administration. In 1963 or early 1964 the Ministry brought together, for the first time in this form, reports[3] on all its investments. In the

[1] Ministry of Waqfs 1964*b*, pp. 183, 186.
[2] Ministry of Waqfs 1964*b*, p. 185.
[3] Ministry of Waqfs, *Al-istithmārāt*, p. 3.

early 1960s the Ministry adopted a general plan to systematize its work on the basis of studies of its functions and responsibilities; accordingly, it collected and arranged all available information concerning its investments. The surplus from which such investments were made was exhausted in the late 1960s.

The Ministry in 1963 held bonds worth nearly £E 5,400,000 which earned interest at the rate of 3·24 per cent. It held shares in government companies totaling more than £E 1,300,000, most of which did not draw a profit; the rate of profit on those which did draw one was 5·12 per cent, while the rate for all shares, including those not making a profit, was 2 per cent. Thus the Ministry held about £E6,700,000 in bonds and shares, plus several other lesser investments amounting to about £E 350,000, yielding a grand total of investments just over £E 7,000,000.

The £E 5,400,000 in bonds in 1963 had a market value about 9 per cent less than that amount. Loans to the government for the development of production made up 72 per cent of all bond purchases by the Ministry. Of the Ministry's £E 1,300,000 in governmental company shares, most (about £E 1,000,000) was in shares listed on the stock exchange; their market value was 29 per cent below their purchase price. Of these £E 1,000,000 of shares, about 37 per cent was in shares yielding no profit at all. This division reflects the general decline in share prices on the market in the 1950s.[1] Most of the profit-yielding shares (some listed on the market and some not) were in banking, textiles, iron and steel, and food. Most of the shares yielding no profit were in chemicals and milk.[2]

In making these investments, the Ministry has acted out of a desire to improve its own financial position and to partici-

---

[1] These figures are taken or calculated from *ibid.* pp. 4–6.
[2] *Ibid.* pp. 73–4.

pate in the national effort to increase production. Statements to this effect appear in many of the Ministry's memorandums reporting its investments. Thus in 1956 it invested £E500,000 in the Egyptian Chemical Industries Company, commenting that the establishment of this enterprise was 'something the Ministry of Waqfs believes in and deems part of its mission in investment and production...'[1]

In the same year the Ministry, in participating in a government bond issue to the extent of £E750,000, observed that such 'exalted patriotic action is incumbent upon every Egyptian'.[2] In 1961 the Ministry, in selling £E750,000 of government bonds to the Treasury to aid in financing housing, pointed out that 'since the beginning of the era of the blessed revolution' it had invested for profit and the national interest more than £E6,000,000 of its surplus funds, leaving itself only enough to meet 'normal obligations'. This policy, it was concluded, meant 'increasing the assets of the Ministry and buttressing the economy of the country'.[3] This investment power has been severely curbed in recent years and has been assimilated to the general planning functions of other governmental agencies.

The Ministry held much larger amounts of money in land and buildings, but it did not systematically arrange these holdings. Incidentally, there has been little public discussion of whether or not returns from company shares are forbidden as interest; the assumption has been made that returns from public corporations, unlike those from private firms, are not really interest. A late head of Al-Azhar, in a legal opinion, held that the prohibition against interest is suspended when the government needs to borrow for the good of the nation.[4] In the case of the investments mentioned above, one government agency was lending to another.

---

[1] *Ibid.* p. 89.
[3] *Ibid.* p. 116.
[2] *Ibid.* p. 91.
[4] Shaltūt, pp. 353–5.

Religious organization

The third chief function of the Ministry of Waqfs, administration of mosques, I have already discussed in some detail. This function is the only one that has appreciably grown in magnitude and significance, for the military regime has entrusted to the Ministry the tasks of improving the condition and services of the mosques and of bringing them more securely within the system of governmental influence upon attitudes and behavior of the population in accordance with the regime's own goals. The mosque and the institutions built up in connection with it must be of utmost significance to a regime bent upon vast social change through forced mobilization of a population devoted to its religious traditions. The mosque has often been the scene of politically important activities; this gives a regime precedent for using the mosque politically, but this tradition also supplies precedent to those who want to resist or withdraw from pressure exerted by foreign or local rulers. I have noticed, and have been told by many persons, that people fill the mosques in troubled times such as Egypt has been passing through. Whether for solace, for withdrawal, or for implied disapproval of governmental policies, the mosque is the one free gathering-place that any regime would hesitate to deny to people. A regime that was suspicious of even the limited opportunity the mosque offers for expression of popular sentiment would seek to control what happens there rather than to prevent people from using it altogether. As the only place where large numbers of people may at present gather freely and without specific official permission in advance, the mosque in Egypt necessarily assumes considerable importance to the military regime.

Governmental policy regarding the mosque, as we have seen, looks to its improvement through raising the standards of governmental mosques and, since 1960, the conversion of private mosques into governmental ones. Governmental concern about mosque conditions was forcefully expressed before the revolution of 1952. The Sanitation Committee for Mosque Improvement in 1942 called the mosque a 'public utility' like schools and hospitals and claimed that hence the state must assume some degree of responsibility for it and not leave its condition to the uncertain impulses of private benefactors. Even more pointedly, the Committee asserted that the Ministry of Waqfs, in its capacity as the exclusive supervisor of mosques, could even 'abolish private mosques that are useless or not in harmony with the public utility concept.'[1]

A generation later, the Ministry, in surveying private mosques in 1964, called attention to the same deficiencies. Whereas the 1942 committee, however, spoke primarily of the religious function of mosques and their sanitary facilities in relation to the public utility concept, in 1964 the Ministry spoke primarily of the role of the mosque in national 'orientation' and only secondarily about their condition. It called for plans to reconstruct the hundreds of mosques not fit for religious services and for improvement of hygienic conditions in thousands of others through cooperation among the central government, local governments and the people. The Ministry also pointed to the need to improve the private mosques because they are places of worship whose good condition every believer regards as even more important than his own welfare.[2] It was aware, too, that the existence of some 14,000 private mosques, compared to only about 3,000 governmental mosques, was the best testimony to popular love and sacrifice 'for the religion of Allah and the love of all that it calls for'. But the commentary soon went on to ideological matters: the large number of private mosques is of great importance in 'national orientation and the dissemi-

---

[1] Sanitation Committee, pp. 1–2.
[2] Ministry of Waqfs 1964*a*, pp. 69–70, 71.

nation of Islamic teachings and the foundations of Islamic socialism'. The government must therefore guide the mosques so that they might become the 'source of spiritual mobilization for the largest number of people.' Left to 'improvisation' and chance, these private mosques are not properly led, with consequent poor guidance in both the 'religious and the patriotic domains.' The Ministry, in addition to taking over private mosques, suggested for those not yet annexed an interim measure: the creation of administrative councils to guide them and to reform their lectures and sermons.[1]

It is indeed possible that the condition of many private mosques has deteriorated in recent years with the decline in the number of persons with large incomes who have traditionally supported them. Recent governmental efforts to improve the conditions of mosques have also stressed the adaptation of the mosque to 'modern' needs. Thus a vice-president of the Republic (one of the original members of the group that led the overthrow of the monarchy in 1952) told a cabinet meeting in 1968 that the mosque should regain its leadership in the community by helping to provide education, medical service, and social guidance for the populace. To do so, he went on, the mosque imams need new specialized training. Mosque, state, and community, according to the plans outlined, would be closely associated under the government's guidance. This was only proper, he suggested, for government originated in the mosque and now that government had expanded and become independent, it must help the mosque to re-establish itself in the modern world.[2]

How has the annexation program developed? Since the government was avowedly interested in raising the level of

[1] *Ibid.* pp. 68–9.
[2] Vice-President Hussein al-Shafei quoted in *Akhbār al-yawm* (Cairo), 13 April 1968, p. 12. On similar plans in the early 1960s, see Crecelius, pp. 43–4.

the private mosques, one might assume that it would annex first the ones most in need of improvement. The fact is, however, that the Ministry of Waqfs began by annexing the private mosques in the best physical and financial condition; these mosques were also in better physical condition than the mosques already owned by the government.

In 1962 there were 2,997 governmental mosques. Of these, 1,322, or 44 per cent, had been taken over from private management only in the previous decade under laws of 1953 and 1960.[1] (These additions probably account for most of the 80 per cent increase in governmental mosque personnel from 1951 to 1963, as shown table 16 above.) The government meanwhile, from 1952 to 1964, built only 78 mosques, at a total cost of £E1,400,000, or an average of about £E18,000 per mosque. In this period, too, the government contributed £E1,235,000 toward the completion of 1,560 private mosques; this is an average of less than 800 pounds per private mosque aided, compared with the average cost of £E18,000 per governmental mosque built.[2]

The surveys of governmental and private mosques permit us to draw up a profile of the private mosques taken over by the government; of 1,100 such mosques, we have information on 679 taken over up to the time of the survey in 1962. How do these private mosques which the government chose to annex first compare to the private mosques it passed by and to those mosques which had already been governmental? The private mosques which the government annexed were superior to the other two, as the following tables will show. These tables compare the three types of mosque: 'public'— those originally governmental, totaling 1,606; 'annexed'— the 679 private mosques taken over by the government in accordance with the law of 1960; and 'private'—the 14,212

---

[1] Ministry of Waqfs 1963, pp. ii (*b*), and 2.
[2] Ministry of Waqfs 1964*b*, p. 73.

private mosques remaining. (In one of the tables these numbers are slightly different.)

Table 18 shows that 82 per cent of the annexed mosques were perfectly sound, compared with 72 per cent and 71 per cent, respectively, of the public and private mosques. It is of course possible that the annexed mosques were not fully sound at the time they were taken over and that they were made so after their annexation. This is not likely, however, because the annexation policy was in force only two years or so at the time of the survey, hardly enough time to change the physical state of so many structures.

As to sanitary facilities, table 19 shows that 63 per cent of the annexed mosques were in good condition and were numerous enough, compared with only 51 per cent of the public mosques and 44 per cent of the private ones that were rated in this highest position.

Another indication of the government's initial policy of annexing the better and more imposing private mosques is shown in table 20. 'Excellent' seems to refer to both size and high quality, while the other catagories refer to size only. Of the annexed mosques, 6 per cent were 'excellent'; this proportion is higher than the 4 per cent for private mosques but lower than the 9 per cent for public mosques. Large mosques among the annexed group, however, were proportionately greater than among the other two groups.

The same pattern is repeated for age, as shown in table 21. Of the public and private mosques 14 per cent and 30 per cent, respectively, were less than thirty years old, but 41 per cent of the annexed mosques were in these two youngest categories. Very likely, the fact that the annexed mosques are newer is correlated with their better physical condition as well.

One other comparison may be relevant: the educational qualifications of the imam, the chief mosque official. Table 22

TABLE 18. *Comparative state of repair of three types of mosque*
(In percentages)

Type of mosque	Good	Fully reparable	Partly reparable	Totally irreparable	Not reported	Total
Annexed	82	8	4	—	6	100
Public	72	13	3	8	4	100
Private	71	9	3	2	15	100

Sources. Annexed and public mosques—Ministry of Waqfs 1963, p. 102.
Private mosques—Ministry of Waqfs 1964a, p. 43.

TABLE 19. *Comparative condition[a] of public conveniences in three types of mosque*
(in percentages)

Type of mosque	Good and sufficient	Good but not sufficient	Not good	None found	Not known	Total
Annexed	63	16	10	3	8	100
Public	51	17	14	5	13	100
Private	44	14	11	7	24	100

[a] 'Good' refers to condition of the conveniences; 'sufficient' refers to their number in relation to need.

Sources: Annexed and public mosques—Ministry of Waqfs 1963, p. 104.
Private mosques—Ministry of Waqfs 1964a, p. 57.

TABLE 20. *Comparative size of three types of mosque*

(in percentages)

Type of mosque	Excellent[a]	Large	Medium	Small	Not reported	Total
Annexed	6	29	38	11	16	100
Public	9	22	35	24	10	100
Private	4	15	41	23	17	100

[a] *mumtāz*.

Sources: Annexed and public mosques—Ministry of Waqfs 1963, pp. 138, 140.
Private mosques—Ministry of Waqfs 1964a, p. 41.

TABLE 21. *Comparative age of three types of mosque*

(in percentages)

Type of mosque	Under 10 years	10–29 years	30 years and over	Not known	Total
Annexed	13	28	51	8	100
Public	5	9	78	8	100
Private	11	19	54	16	100

Sources: Annexed and public mosques—Ministry of Waqfs 1963, p. 101.
Private mosques—Ministry of Waqfs 1964a, p. 42.

TABLE 22. *Comparison of educational qualifications of imams in three types of mosque*

(in percentages)

Type of mosque	High	Inter-mediate	Below inter-mediate	None	Total
Annexed	21	20	17	42	100
Public	71	16	6	7	100
Private	2	6	13	79	100

Sources: Annexed and public mosques—Ministry of Waqfs 1963, p. 6, table 1. Private mosques—Ministry of Waqfs 1964*a*, p. 9.

shows that the proportion of imams in the public mosques who have a higher degree is 71 per cent, far greater than that in the other two types. The proportion for the annexed mosques is 21 per cent, far higher than that for private mosques. This may be because the government selected for annexation those mosques that had better leadership, or perhaps the government assigned highly trained imams to the annexed mosques once they were taken over. No definitive judgment is possible on the basis of available data. It may be, then, that in this case annexation led to more capable mosque leadership.

This practice of government annexation of the better mosques is clearly established by these comparisons. As we shall see in Chapter 4, the government engaged in a similar practice with respect to the voluntary charitable organizations. Such practice, indeed, parallels governmental take-overs in the economic realm as well; it has for years been more ready to annex profitable private enterprises than unprofitable ones (size, public importance and other relevant factors being equal).

Our conclusion must be that the military regime, if it has not opposed religion as such, has sought to induce the masses to see beyond religion or to see religion differently—to see it as the regime would like to use it: to buttress nationalism, socialism and the one-party 'popular democracy'. In this effort the regime has followed two policies. First, it has put the somewhat autonomous religious institutions and associations of the people under the supervision of the Ministry of Waqfs. Second, it has transferred such governmental power as can be exerted over religion from the traditionalist Ministry of Waqfs to other agencies more responsive to the new goals. In making religion an instrument of the state, the government has also sought some genuine reforms in religious organization and practice, following a long tradition of such efforts; but this goal has been clearly secondary and progress toward it rather limited.

3

Aspects of
sufi organization
and activity

A great deal has been written about sufi doctrine in the past but very little on sufi organization and activity today or in this century. This lack is particularly unfortunate because in Egypt there are still many active sufi orders each commanding the loyalty of many thousands of members and other followers. We know little about these people and their organizations. It may be argued that we do not need to know much about them because they are no longer important in religion and politics. Although this may be true (but without study how can we know?), their influence may still be considerable, although perhaps expressed differently today. In any case, if we are interested in contemporary social life we cannot continue to ignore this aspect of popular religious belief and conduct.

My purpose, therefore, is first to describe aspects of present-day sufi organization and appeal in Egypt on the basis of some documents, my observation of sufi activities, and my interviews with sufis; and secondly to raise some questions about these matters in order to show that this neglected field is worthy of scholarly empirical study.

Aspects of sufi organization

BACKGROUND OF SUFISM

There is unfortunately no adequate social history of sufism in general, nor are there more than a few accounts of the organization and activity of specific orders or of the place of sufism in a particular country.[1]

Since early in Islam, sufism has been practiced in more than a hundred important brotherhoods or orders (ṭarīqa, pl. ṭuruq). The brotherhood was usually founded by a religious teacher or scholar who attracted followers by his piety and asceticism. Many such founders, believed to have hidden powers, have been worshipped as saints. The followers have built a common life in monasteries and neighborhoods, with a hierarchy for administration of the group's various functions such as guidance in the doctrine and practice of asceticism and mysticism, education, and welfare. The brotherhoods have elaborated a rich ceremonial life of prayer, religious enthusiasm and ecstasy, pilgrimages to the tombs of founders and colorful birthday celebrations (mawlids) to honor saintly founders. With the advent of secularism in government and education, and modern cities and industry, the sufi orders have declined in number, membership and political power. Governments have tried, with varying degrees, to suppress them. Many orders have been accused of degeneration into exhibitionism by the members and corrupt acts by the leaders. Yet in Egypt hundreds of thousands of

---

[1] It is worth noting some exceptions and some traditional sources. Late nineteenth-century Algeria is well surveyed by Depont and Coppolani, although from the viewpoint of French control of dissident groups. A good recent North African study has been made of the Tijaniya by Abun-Nasr. For Egypt, Lane (Chapter x) and Mubārak (*passim*) give information for the nineteenth century, Kahle early in the twentieth, and recently Taftazānī and Gilsenan have given brief general reviews of the present situation. Gramlich gives a good summary of the Persian orders, Lewis (1961), pp. 398–418, gives a brief but informative review of the political role of the orders in Turkey since the nineteenth century. See also the articles on Darwīsh and Futuwwa in *E.I.*[2] and Ṭarīḳa in *Shorter E.I.*

rural and urban people are still so deeply committed to the sufi 'way' or 'path' (the primary meaning of ṭarīqa) that anyone interested in social life today must take account of them and seek to understand their continuing appeal.

Although sufi doctrines very early became reconciled with Islamic theology, and although the sufi orders have been important in popular Islam for many centuries, there has been much discussion both among Muslim thinkers and Western Orientalists as to whether or not sufism is 'inherent' in Islam. Muslims who dislike its 'excesses' have armed themselves with appropriate quotations from the Koran and the traditions and insisted that sufism is alien to Islam. Some Western observers, considering sufism a noble achievement, readily agree, and go on to claim that it came to Islam from Christianity.[1] The most authoritative Western views among Orientalists, however, are rather balanced. Gibb pointed out that sufism could not be easily repressed because it was 'too firmly based on the Koran and the moral teachings of Islam' and it satisfied the 'religious instincts of the people, instincts which were to some extent chilled and starved by the abstract and impersonal teachings of the orthodox and found relief in the more directly personal and emotional approach' of sufism.[2] Nicholson referred to Ibn Khaldun's dictum that sufism was 'born in Islam' and concluded that its principles were practiced by the first Muslims; if sufism was a reaction against Islamic formalism, he implies, it was itself an Islamic reaction despite 'the part which Christain influence must have had in shaping' early sufi doctrines.[3] Goldziher regarded asceticism as an integral part of Islam, and Macdonald held the same view of mysticism.[4] In any case, sufi doctrine and practice have been so thoroughly a part of Islam that those

[1] For example, Smith, p. 124.   [2] Gibb, p. 135.
[3] Nicholson, pp. 229–31.
[4] Goldziher, p. 111; Macdonald, p. 113.

who deny the connection seem to do so on the basis of a moral rather than historical assessment.

The most accurate way to put the matter, it seems to me, is to say that sufism is an unorthodox yet characteristically Islamic response to a need left unfulfilled by orthodoxy. Although unorthodox in some formal sense, sufi orders were among Islam's most enthusiastic and virile agencies for winning converts. On the borderlands of Islam the orders, combining asceticism, withdrawal, and militant advocacy, have been psychologically and materially well equipped to proselytize. Is the unorthodox or incompletely integrated advocate of a religious or political faith the most resourceful persuader? Sufism's success in this domain probably stems from (1) its willingness to adjust to the traditions and needs of proselytes, since sufism itself held to no very rigid system, (2) its intimate quality as a form of religion and the charismatic character of its leaders, and (3) its alienation from the religious establishment, ranging from distrust to open opposition.

Unorthodoxy and a pliant spirit in proselytization both reveal a certain sufi tolerance for strange ideas and conduct that incites purist reactions such as Wahhabism. The 'cleansing' movements in Islam have vigorously opposed sufism as shi'ite or 'Alid tendencies given to veneration of saints and other practices not in consonance with Islam in its pristine state. The service the sufi orders gave to Islam could not, however, be denied, all the more as the sufis not only won converts but also proved themselves to be among the most effective defenders of the Islamic communities against the encroachments of Europe and Christianity.

For all its vigor in proselytization and defense against the West in the border zones, internally sufism was politically unreliable. This tendency to subversion had two sources: the sufis challenged the orthodox, state-affiliated religious leaders on theological grounds; and some orders gathered the support of numbers chiefly from the poorer classes, while in some places and eras retaining connections with other groups, not established or fully controlled by the state, such as guilds and young men's associations.[1] With the European conquests of Muslim lands, the sufis turned to resistance to foreign as well as domestic rule. In the late nineteenth century Depont and Coppolani expressed the colonial view of the Algerian brotherhoods' internal and external political role. Under the color of divine inspiration, these authors remarked, the brotherhoods consolidated their own temporal power. From their religious strongholds (zāwiyas) blew a 'perpetual wind of rebellion' against all government. France, they said, could not permit such centers of revolt to exist, not could it allow resources which it controlled to be used against French authority. The authors summarized the political role of the brotherhoods in this way: 'They are by nature enemies of all established authority; and Muslim states as well as European powers governing Muslims must reckon with these antisocial preachers.'[2]

We have mentioned three paradoxical aspects of the social history of sufism. First, sufism became a conventional and characteristically Islamic response to Islamic orthodoxy. Second, although unorthodox and hence theologically rebellious, sufis were among the most earnest and vigorous proselytizers of Islam. Third, although they were effective proselytizers among unbelievers and defenders of the faith against European-Christian encroachment upon Muslim lands, the sufis continued to be internal rebels against Muslim rulers. The final paradox is that sufism should have posed so profound a threat when its entire impulse lay in withdrawal from social life into asceticism, mysticism, and an isolated form of fellowship.

---

[1] The political role and affiliations of medieval sufism are discussed in Lewis 1937; Nicholson, pp. 463–4; Gibb, pp. 134–5; Rahman, pp. 151–2; Kissling; article on Futuwwa in *E.I.*[2].

[2] Depont and Coppolani, pp. 231–2, xiii.

Aspects of sufi organization

The paradoxes are still not exhausted. An unstable element in the organization of political power by both domestic and foreign rulers, sufi orders have themselves been surprisingly stable in internal organization. Based on volatile personal attitudes demanding considerable individual freedom in religion, the orders have been dominated by charismatic leaders; yet some have been able to construct enduring hierarchies and loyalties—in a word, an orthodoxy of their own. Having survived inner turbulence, many orders in Egypt now can trace their origins back several centuries. It may indeed be their loose organization that has enabled them to endure so long, despite the inherent volatility of the teacher–disciple relationship. It appears that the impulses to and advantages of association outweigh the tendency to divide on the basis of minor doctrinal distinctions and personal loyalties. As Depont and Coppolani noted at the turn of this century: 'The formation of these various societies derives its earliest origins from the Muslims' tendency to association, a tendency whose own source is the religious faith which prescribes that they should combine and share with their brothers the goods that God has granted.'[1] The instability of a given sufi group at any particular moment should remind us, as Fazlur Rahman has recently pointed out, that the later translation of ṭarīqa as a brotherhood or order gives a little too strong an organizational sense to a word which originally meant and still means a 'way' or 'path,' that is, a mode of conduct rather than a formal association.[2]

In late 1964 I was given the names of sixty-four functioning sufi orders in Egypt, all of them represented in the Supreme Sufi Council (al-majlis al-ṣūfī al-ʿalā). In 1958, the Council

---

[1] Depont and Coppolani, p. x.   [2] Rahman, pp. 156–7.

5-2

listed sixty orders, including one not in the later list given
me.[1] The formal structure of government within the orders
as well as relations among them have not materially changed
since the nineteenth century. The basic statute is still a
khedivial decree of 1903, which fixes the Council's jurisdic-
tion and makeup.[2] The Head of the Council was appointed
by the khedive under nominal Ottoman rule, then by the
king, and that power is now reserved for the president of the
Republic. The Head of the Council selects the other four
members from among eight sheikhs nominated every three
years by the general assembly of the heads of all the sufi orders.
Even the language used to describe this organization has not
materially changed from the decree issued in 1903, when
Egypt was occupied by the British but nominally ruled by a
khedive in the name of the Ottoman sultan, to the guide to
sufism issued by the Council in 1958, six years after the advent
of the military republican regime. The decree stipulates, in
article 5, that the Council's rules are binding on all sufi orders
whether or not they are officially recognized. The Council
itself is bound to act in accordance with sufi rules, provided
these do not violate the sharī'a.

The hierarchy within the sufi order has not changed much
either, judging from the description by Depont and Coppolani in 1897 and that of the Supreme Sufi Council of Egypt in
1958.[3] At the head of each order is the shaikh, who has complete authority in all respects over the entire order and all its
affairs. He has a representative (nā'ib) in the chief localities
where he has followers. The next official is the naqīb, a direct
link between the shaikh and his followers in respect to administration and ceremonials. There is at least one naqīb in
the order's headquarters and each nā'ib usually has one also.

---

[1] 'Ulwān, pp. 71–4.
[2] *Egyptian Official Gazette* (*Al-waqā'i' al-Miṣrīya*), No. 61, 3 June 1903, p. 997.
[3] Depont and Coppolani, pp. 193–5, 204–5; 'Ulwān, pp. 68–9.

Perhaps the most important official is the khalīfa, the shaikh's deputy for religious functions in the various localities and the effective head of the individual section of the order. Finally there are the murīdūn, the shaikh's disciples and regular members of the order. Most orders are controlled from the headquarters in Cairo; but the activity of the members—the chief purpose and function of the order—is local activity under the khalīfa and nā'ib. These officials are in frequent contact with the shaikh in headquarters, in other large cities, or in the smaller localities which the shaikh visits usually at least once a year.

For the late nineteenth century in Algeria, Depont and Coppolani were able to provide details of the financing of the orders that are seldom found today. They reported that in 1896 the orders received from their members seven and a half million francs (not including the value of their forced or voluntary labor and irregular gifts), which was nearly half the amount of the tax yield to the government from the Algerian (non-European) population.[1] The orders in Egypt today are still supported mainly by the members and by small contributions from the government. The decline of private wealth has virtually eliminated the rich donors who formerly contributed large sums. Historically, the Ministry of the Interior acted for the government in certain sufi matters, and this arrangement still prevails with respect to the election of the Supreme Sufi Council, the organization and conduct of the annual birthday celebrations (which bring together vast numbers of people and affect public order), and the election of the shaikhs of three of the orders.

It is widely believed in Egypt that the post of the head of all sufi orders there (shaikh mashāyikh) was established by Saladin. Depont and Coppolani asserted that it was Muhammad Ali who created this post in order better to control the

---

[1] Depont and Coppolani, pp. 242–4.

orders. Gibb and Bowen likewise place the creation of the post in the nineteenth century.[1] An Egyptian student of the orders, however, argues that the post did not exist formally during Ottoman times in Egypt nor at any time before that. From time to time, one sufi leader or another achieved enough influence to exercise informal leadership of all of them. The formal post of head of all the orders, however, he finds to be rather recent.[2] It may thus be only in the early part of this century that it was established in its present form. The power of the sufi shaikhs of the influential orders was, however, admittedly great even if there was none that spoke for all. The same writer reviews some evidence showing that in Ottoman times sufi shaikhs were rather independent of the rulers of Egypt, were able to challenge state power, enjoyed the respect of rulers, and brooked no interference from the state in governing the members of their own orders. They thus protected their members from the tyranny of central government; and the members were more loyal to their religious sufi leaders than to the more distant state.[3] On their side, the rulers of the state sought the help of the shaikhs both in deference to religious piety and authority and in the hope of avoiding conflict with the powerful orders.[4]

All this is in stark contrast to the political position of the sufi orders today. Their internal regimes are probably more stable, but at the price of submission to the greater power of the central government in the broad domain in which religion touches politics. The guide to sufism published in 1958 by the Supreme Sufi Council thus hailed the 'blessed revolution' of 1952 as the great hope for the nation. This attitude is not surprising, because it is one that was widely held throughout the country. The Council, however, referred

---

[1] Depont and Coppolani, p. 262; Gibb and Bowen, p. 199.
[2] Al-Ṭawīl, pp. 99, 102–3.
[3] *Ibid.* pp. 117, 119–20, 167. [4] *Ibid.* p. 137.

also to the orders' revival of spirit and activity, which it attributed to 'God's blessing and support and to the encouragement and help of the Revolution and its great leader.'[1] This was probably more prudent hyperbole than anything else, yet its nature and direction clearly indicated the movement's pliancy. The Council's political reliability has been demonstrated on specific matters as well; one of the most recent examples was its attack upon the Muslim Brotherhood in 1965 when it was accused of a terrorist conspiracy against the regime.[2]

Historically it appears that the political decline of the orders proceeded independently of excesses of their ceremonials. In Lane's time, for example, the orders were still powerful, yet he discussed them under the heading of 'superstitions.'[3] Early in this century Macdonald described an effort to keep the sufis from making spectacles of themselves. 'It is exceedingly difficult, now,' he told an American audience in 1909 concerning his stay in Egypt the previous year, 'to get admission to any of their religious services. At one time, . . . these were crowded with tourists. That led to scandal. The darwīshes were accused of making money out of the unbelievers. . . At last the government stepped in, acting through the Shaykh al-Bekri as the head of all the fraternities, and these services were closed to all except Muslims. So far as the Shaykh al-Bekri was concerned, he would have preferred to stop the services entirely, but that was impossible.'[4] In 1958 the Supreme Sufi Council itself referred to sufism's

---

[1] 'Ulwān, p. 54.   [2] *Al-Akhbār* (Cairo), 1 October 1965, p. 6.
[3] Lane, Chapter x. It is worth recalling Lane's incidental comment in that discussion (p. 241): 'It is a very remarkable trait in the character of the people of Egypt and other countries of the East, that Muslims, Christians, and Jews adopt each other's superstitions, while they abhor the leading doctrines of each other's faiths.'
[4] Macdonald, p. 160. An account of the religious and secular sides of these popular celebrations in the period before World War II is given by McPherson, Chapters III and IV.

degeneration into mere ceremonial and spectacle.[1] Macdonald found early in this century what I found more than half a century later, that many Muslims are scandalized by a Westerner's interest (even if described as scholarly) in the activities of the sufi orders.[2]

In the early 1950s, the military regime had hopes of changing the orders, to impress them into serving its goals of industrialization and 'modernization'. As organizations of hundreds of thousands of poor people, the orders could be viewed as either an instrument or a potential threat. The government now seems to have become resigned to letting the orders go their own way; since they pose no immediate political challenge, they may be viewed as a harmless emotional outlet. The regime would doubtless prefer to have the orders' active and effective cooperation, but that seems to be too much to expect. Some of the orders are led by shaikhs and khalīfas who seek to introduce them to more modern education, hygiene and even to the discipline of modern industry. The head of the order of Al-Ghunaimīya al-Khalwatīya, a member of the Supreme Sufi Council, for example, has a Ph.D. and is a member of the philosophy department of the University of Cairo. On the whole, however, the 'modernizers' have abandoned hope for the sufis, whose inclinations and activities are said to make them useless in or irrelevant to modern life. The government's encouragement of a certain kind of political activity and workers' participation in management does not, however, seem to have been much more successful in fitting the mass of the population for modern industry. Political distractions seem to have blocked this process in recent years just as religious distractions may have blocked it in previous eras.

[1] 'Ulwān, p. 54.
[2] Macdonald, p. 50.

Aspects of sufi organization

For a long time writers on sufism have been saying that its appeal lies in the comradeship and drama it offers in contrast to the formality of Islamic orthodoxy. Thus Evans-Pritchard said of the urban orders in Cyrenaica: 'They provide the only spontaneous and cooperative associations in the towns and thus fill a gap for ordinary people both in the town society and in a religion which pays little attention either to corporeal works or, outside the mosques, to corporate worship.'[1] The tension between 'folk' and 'formal' elements, which appeared early in Islam, is of course found in other religions and goes back to early times. The desire for spontaneity and autonomy takes various forms. In the United States of America today, for example, Catholic masses conducted in private homes are becoming more and more frequent. A newspaper account describes their appeal in terms usually found in descriptions of sufi orders: 'In practically all cases, home masses grow out of a search for a more "personal" or "intimate" form of worship than is available in large Sunday masses in local parishes.'[2] And in Egypt today there are several comparable manifestations of a need for religious spontaneity. About twenty years ago there was a revival of interest in communication with the dead; recently it has spread to many educated people and to intellectuals, who take it seriously either as a form of traditional mysticism or an alternative to it. In April 1968 many people asserted that they saw the form of the Virgin Mary above a church in the Zeitoun district of Cairo; thousands of people, Muslims as well as Christians, spent many hours there daily after sundown in the hope of seeing the Virgin or of simply participating in the excitement. On several evenings in early May I saw hundreds of thousands of

[1] Evans-Pritchard, p. 87.
[2] *The New York Times*, 20 May 1968, p. 49.

amiable people expectantly milling about in the area of the modest church.[1] Finally, many educated men have recently become greatly interested in several aspects of religion. Professors, judges, higher civil servants and army officers have been meeting spontaneously and unobtrusively in mosques and private homes to read the Koran together, discuss mysticism and even to perform the famous dhikr (literally, the mentioning, i.e., rhythmic repetition of God's name in certain phrases—a sufi ritual). Such groups seem to have increased considerably in the last decade or so.

Why does sufism continue to revive even in the midst of what is called a general decline? It is not enough to say that it is inherent in Islam, for that does not help us to understand changes in the position of sufism and the orders. Nor does it carry us far to say that sufism is itself a sign of cultural decline[2] or, for that matter, of revival. Sufism is certainly related to such broad movements of culture but it is too simple to call it a touchstone to everything human.

Sufi orders were first established nearly a thousand years ago in religious, political and economic settings that have changed considerably in the last century or two. The orders flourished during a long period when religious ideas were more influential than now in social relations, when state power was less pervasive, and when men worked in smaller and more autonomous economic units. As changes took place, the mutually supporting connections which the orders enjoyed with other associations and institutions became weaker (the exact process, however, has not yet been adequately described by scholars). Despite the orders' decline in political power and economic relevance, they still perform religious and other social functions (likewise inadequately

[1] See also *The New York Times*, 11 August 1968, p. 4.
[2] Meier, pp. 221–2, rejects the idea that sufism itself symbolizes cultural decline.

studied), but in a vastly different setting. The very broad social needs that first impelled Muslims to follow sufism and to establish the orders may be much the same today: desire for spontaneity, warmth, intimacy, and so on. But the practice of sufism and the position of the orders today require their own explanation aside from their origin and the possibility that they fulfill social needs that may have been broadly similar throughout the history of the movement. Several hypotheses suggest themselves.

First, Egypt has undergone considerable social stress in this century. Since around 1952 the government has taken the lead in seeking to transform the nation, including its religious attitudes and behavior. Within a decade or so, republican Egypt has been twice defeated in wars with Israel involving issues to which the regime has attached the highest importance and on which it has tried to arouse the nation to extraordinary efforts. The expectations of internal social and economic progress have not been realized. Dissent has not been allowed to express itself. In such conditions of rapid political change, stress, unachieved goals and denial of free expression it seems natural that a religious people should turn to that form of solidarity still permitted to it.[1] During Ramadan a few months after the war of June 1967, for example, the government-owned press published more religious discussion than in previous annual observances of this holy month.

Second, long-range changes in the direction of modern industry and urbanization may have weakened the kinship structure and induced men to seek solidarity by returning to

---

[1] A student of Egyptian sufi history has presented this hypothesis. He explains the flourishing of sufism in Egypt in the thirteenth century A.D. as a response to oppression, defeat in war, immorality, irreligion, and poverty. These conditions stirred pious men to preach a return to religion and self-sacrifice, and they won over many people disturbed and frustrated in such times. See Ḥusain, Chapter 2. The poverty and compensation themes are given also for a later period by the historian, El-Shayyal, p. 125.

75

traditional religious brotherhoods but out of different impulses from those that may have been dominant in earlier eras.

Third, if sufism has traditionally been a reaction against strict orthodoxy, it is to be expected that it would provide a haven today in Egypt where the government, as we saw in Chapter 2, has steadily reduced the autonomy of even the official religious establishment.

Fourth, the regime's efforts to supply secular opportunities for spontaneity and autonomy, such as television and other entertainment media, trade unions, a mass political party with no rivals, and rigidly-controlled cultural clubs,[1] have perhaps not only failed but have indeed impelled people to find genuinely autonomous associations that have deep roots and that are not proscribed (even if not encouraged).

These hypotheses are of course not mutually exclusive; they may be encompassed in one broad notion that social stress and a strong authoritarian trend have sent people searching for relief in those few corners of social life where self-direction, trust and intimacy are still possible. The trouble is that not only do we lack an adequate social history of sufi orders but we also lack contemporary studies bearing on these (or other) hypotheses. In view of this lack, I regard it as worth-while to offer some personal observations, not so much as evidence for these hypotheses but as elucidations of them.

Although sufism is considered a form of popular religion, it has its own 'high' and 'low' forms, which have become increasingly separated in the current revival in Egypt. On the one hand are the mass of the followers in the orders, who have little formal education, work at menial jobs, obey their shaikhs unquestioningly, and participate fully in the overt and ceremonial aspects of the orders' activities.[2] On the other

[1] E.g., see Gilsenan, p. 16.
[2] A few years ago an Egyptian social scientist published a study of the letters of complaint and supplication addressed through the post to the famous

hand, I met many well-educated Egyptians who have adopted or resumed an interest in sufi ideas; some spent several years in Western countries as students or government officials. Their interest is in doctrine and meditation for themselves and in social welfare in the orders—i.e., a deeper form of religious devotion and brotherhoood than they can experience elsewhere.[1]

It is instructive to compare the attitudes of these highly educated, successful men attracted to sufism with those of successful men with somewhat less education who are repelled by it. Though I spoke at length with many men of both groups, I made no attempt at a systematic attitude-opinion survey; I shall therefore briefly describe the positions of four real persons (to whom I shall give pseudonyms) whom I regard as broadly representative of both groups, in order to show how some people think about sufism these days.

'Hussein Suleiman' is a high official in the educational system who has studied and served in Western countries. As he approached fifty years of age, he became increasingly interested in religion, though not in an organizational sense. He found many other men of his age and social class who felt the same way. Their interest took the form of a return to regular daily prayer as well as to the Friday prayer in the mosque, a concern for the religious education of their children, giving charity, and an effort to be kind and honorable in personal relations. The men came together informally but

---

Imam al-Shāfiʿī (died 820 A.D.), the founder of one of the four schools of Islamic law. Simple believers sent these letters to the tomb of the Imam in the Cairo mosque named for him. Though not dealing directly with sufism, this study throws light on the attitudes and expectations of the followers of sufi leaders. See ʿUweis.

[1] This distinction between 'high' and 'low' sufism is probably related to but not the same as the one which Moriah, p. 387, describes between two kinds of orders in eighteenth-century Egypt: orthodox orders, associated with 'contemplative and ascetic mysticism'; and 'popular' orders, 'associated mainly with shrine-cult and ecstatic practices'.

frequently; their purpose was not specifically religious but their talk usually turned to religion, which they saw as both a guide in a period of rapid change in attitudes and behavior in their own generation and younger ones, and as a way of re-affirming the worth and relevance of Islam. 'Most of us', 'Dr Suleiman' told me, 'have been to the West and have seen its power and glamor. We don't reject all that, but we feel that for ourselves Islam is a deeper religion and culture. It also helps us to put our Western experience into perspective.' He admitted that two common characteristics could be found in every member of the group: each was in his middle or late forties, and each had some particular personal condition that affected his life profoundly. For himself, that condition was the death of his wife a few years ago, his childlessness, his recent remarriage and the birth of several children to his wife. Sufism entered into the religious behavior of only a few of this group, but it strongly affected 'Hussein Suleiman' himself. His late father had been a sufi and as a boy he had attended sufi ceremonials, so it was natural for him now to turn to sufi treatises in his leisure.

'Rashad Lutfi,' a high official in the foreign office, has likewise had experience in the West. His own turn toward religion is more intellectual and his interest in sufism has been to interpret it in relation to the needs of Muslims today. He stressed the two strains in sufism, the impulse to withdraw from a sinful world and the desire to reform it. The sufism that withdraws, he insisted, is not entirely in harmony with Islam, which is a religon of this world as well as of the next one. The sufism that seeks to make this world conform to the ideal is more truly Islamic, in his view. This reformist approach, however, does not impel him to any activist role in sufi orders; his interest and commitment remain personal and intellectual.

We come now to two men hostile to sufism in any form.

The first is 'Ismail Abbas', a minor official in the accounting department of a Western company doing business in the Middle East. He is therefore familiar with Western ways without ever having been in the West. He sees sufism as more mystification than mysticism; he is repelled by the doctrine, which he regards as anti-Islamic; by the ceremonials, which he considers exhibitionistic and primitive; and by the rank and file of sufis, whom he finds ignorant, dirty, and unproductive. He is himself religious and very critical of Western moral laxity and coldness; yet he often spoke of sufi practices as shameful to Muslims in the eyes of 'civilized' people from other cultures. Repelled by 'low' or 'popular' sufism, he is intellectually and emotionally incapable of being attracted to 'high' sufism either.

The second man is 'Hamed Mustafa', a skilled worker in Western-owned industries who became a trade union leader and then a high government official. As a young worker, he went with a friend to a few sufi meetings. 'In less than a week,' he told me, 'I stopped going. I couldn't stand the acceptance of poverty. Poor people should try to improve themselves in a practical way, instead of absorbing so much religion that they forget their poverty and allow themselves to go around dirty and unaware of what's going on in the world.' Religion, he insisted, must help people in this life to work hard, to educate themselves and to appreciate cleanliness. Although not a Marxist in any genuine ideological sense, he saw sufism as a barrier to the worker's self-understanding; asceticism and mysticism were beyond his comprehension. When 'Hamed Mustafa' held influential posts, he sought to weave religious themes into his efforts to educate workers to their interests, but these themes related to this world and were ancillary to his main goal of material improvement for the industrial worker.

Critics and advocates of sufism have for generations argued

that the orders must reform in order to survive. Committees are formed, speeches made, resolutions passed, but the orders carry on with little change. Proposals are made for the orders to undertake practical work among peasants and workers; the results are negligible. The Supreme Sufi Council itself has joined the chorus calling for change, yet to little or no avail. These failures, it seems to me, have made it clear that sufi orders cannot 'adjust' to 'modern' life and satisfy their members at the same time. The impulses the orders respond to and the needs they supply lie outside the practical, instrumental goals relating to material welfare, which in any case are the concern of other agencies. If the orders were transformed into 'modernizing' agencies, they would ultimately be replaced by other associations seeking to fill the gap such a change would create. It is precisely because they are not practical, are not diverted toward other goals, that the orders are important to those who enlist in them. Early in this century William James expressed this reformist position in a poignant way, for he accepted the value of asceticism and religion. Believers, he said, should not simply oppose or ignore the 'ascetic impulse' but should find a way to make its personal sacrifices socially useful. Was it not possible, he asked, referring mainly to monasticism, 'to discard most of these older forms of mortification, and yet find saner channels for the heroism which inspired them?'[1] The question is quite relevant in Egypt today. The severest critics of the sufi orders are those who see in this energy and activity a force they would like to 'mobilize' for state-proclaimed goals. Why not 'harness' this movement, as private enterprise was 'harnessed' first by state regulation and then by state ownership? Impatient leaders are disturbed, for example, when they see the mawlids, those elaborate celebrations of the birthdays of sufi founders, which consume human energy, time and

[1] James, pp. 356–7 (Chapters XIV–XV).

wealth without contributing to national strength as defined by the holders of state power. These celebrations are directed toward a sense of community that is wider than the state or to individual impulses that are narrower than the state. In any case, the planners cannot fit them into the national accounts.

The mawlid is an affirmation of solidarity conducted today in much the same way as it was centuries ago. Among the mawlids I attended in 1964–5, the one of the order of al-Bayūmīya (a branch of the Ahmadīya) is representative for our present purpose.[1] The main ceremony was built around a procession (zaffa) from the order's headquarters (in the Bāb al-Sha'rīya district of Cairo), along the street named for the order's founder, to the mosque named for him too, where a new turban ('imma) was placed upon his tomb. The headquarters were in a run-down building with an open court. Members gathered there all day, and by evening there were hundreds in all parts of the headquarters, chanting, sitting, standing about as they prepared for the march. Certain members formed themselves into two rows, holding hands and facing each other. Between these rows the mass of the members lined up into four columns, carrying their red banners (the Ahmadīya color), and led by two men carrying two huge drums. The marchers were mostly poorly dressed in the common shirt-like gowns (jalabīya), with an assortment of Western-style jackets and sweaters over them; a few wore Western suits. Most of them appeared to be in their thirties and forties. With a few women and children struggling at the rear, the marchers set off for the founder's mosque a short distance away.

Along the route, a poor section of Cairo, the scene was a mass of humanity, color, movement and din. Electric light

---

[1] For a description of this mawlid in the 1930s and something of its earlier history, see McPherson, pp. 173–8. For a brief general discussion, see the article on Mawlid in *Shorter E.I.*

bulbs forming circular and rectangular designs were strung from side to side at many points along the street that was the line of march. Men, women and children were everywhere, singing, calling aloud, yelling, running, and eating. In the side streets and alleys and at the sides of the houses we passed there were thousands of members praying and chanting in small groups. No one knew or was willing to guess how many thousands of people came to Cairo for the great event, sleeping in cheap hotels, apartment houses, in special open areas roped off from the streets, everywhere a space could be found.

Absolutely everything was open and everyone was in the streets or looking out of windows. All cafes were filled, their radios and loud-speakers blaring. There was religious music, popular music, there were singers and story-tellers. Here and there hundreds of children were enjoying themselves on rickety rides like those found in amusement parks, and all over the masses of children—boys and girls indistin-guishable—ran and yelled, fought and scraped, rolled in water and dirt, forming a dazzling confusion of clothing styles and colors. The shops were wide open—blacksmiths, metal works, groceries, bakeries and innumerable barber shops. In these small spaces scores of workers, customers and hangers-on were cramped and from them dozens of others overflowed into the streets.

As the marchers reached the mosque and filed into it, the confusion of bodies and movement intensified. The mosque was already crowded and a ritual (dhikr) in progress. Around the mosque were the wives and children of the men inside it; many appeared to have been there for a long time, leaning or sleeping against the walls day and night. With their meager possessions they staked out a small circle like bathers on a crowded beach. The poverty was notable even for a poor district of Cairo; many of the children had running sores and were only half-dressed, the women looked old and dry, cripples abounded—all seeking solace or perhaps some miracle for their simple faith in the saintly founder of the order. And through the seething mass around the mosque filtered the calculating peddlers selling fruits, nuts, sweets, cooked foods, combs and other plastic goods, and the pick-pockets able to find something of value even among paupers.

As the ceremony proceeded inside the mosque, hundreds watched it from the outside. Women kissed the walls of the mosque and the iron bars around the glassless windows, and dragged their children to do the same. The ceremony itself produced exaltation, fervor, rapture and in many a tranquil contentment. The turban placed upon the tomb, the main ritual was over. Many people began to drift away, the excite-ment around the mosque abated, and the locus of celebration shifted again to the streets.

Another sufi ceremony I attended was somewhat different. This was the khalwa of the Demirdāshīya order, that is, the ritual at the beginning of the seclusion of some members in small cells along the walls of the order's mosque.[1] The head-quarters and mosque, in the Abbasiya district of Cairo, are an impressive group of connected buildings, all of them well-furnished, clean, and properly maintained. Before the open-ing of the evening ceremony, the mosque was already crowded with people praying in all the corners, small groups of boys playing in an orderly way, and twenty to thirty women and girls squatting along a wall. From the shaikh's office, as preparations were completed, the thirty men there filed into another room off the mosque, where there were a pulpit (minbar) and a microphone. About a hundred and fifty men squatted or kneeled in this room, while several hundred other people remained in the mosque alongside. All were

---

[1] Lane, Chapter x, briefly describes this ceremony as he saw it in the second quarter of the nineteenth century.

6-2

dressed well, mostly in Eastern clothing. In the room, perhaps a quarter of the men wore Western clothing, and of
them four or five were well dressed by the highest European
standard. The first speaker, in a Western suit, read from a
manuscript a rather good history of the order, replete with
names and dates. He spoke with feeling, but as a university
lecturer might, and in excellent Arabic. He was followed by a
passionate orator who aroused the audience to religious fervor. Two more speakers arose to explain the significance of
this day and ceremony. The audience filed into two rooms
set up for dining, one for those who would later go into the
cells, and one for the others. The room for the fasters had no
chairs; on a rug there were about forty settings consisting
simply of a piece of bread on a white napkin. In the other room
settings were on a well-stocked table: silverware, napkins,
baskets of fruit, and an assortment of meats and vegetables.

Following the two meals, grand and humble, the men
about to enter the cells gathered in formation and marched
to the mosque, followed by the others. Each sufi entered his
cell along the mosque wall. The cell was very high, but only
about five feet long and three feet wide. The cell walls were
of cement and the door leading to the mosque was of wood.
The only furnishings were a floor mat and two little shelves
at knee-height for the occupant's personal belongings. The
sufi stays in the cell to meditate and pray, leaving only to use
the toilet and to eat simple food (bread, soup, fruit, beans).
On this occasion the plan was to spend the hours of darkness
in the cell for one week.

ASCETICISM, MYSTICISM AND POLITICS

The khalwa, involving seclusion and self-denial, epitomizes
the sufi way and its divergence from even the religious life of
the rest of society. Asceticism and mysticism, however inte-

gral they may be to the religious practice of Muslims, are
still not congenial to the communal spirit of Islam itself.
Orthodoxy may have little difficulty in tolerating or en-
couraging a mild asceticism, but it certainly cannot be happy
with private mystical experience. We know very little about
the relationship of asceticism and mysticism to the living
world of Muslims today, nor do we know much about the
connections between asceticism and mysticism—why they
coincide and how they combine in different proportions.
Here, too, much research remains to be done, not so much
into doctrine but primarily into the behavior and attitudes of
practicing ascetics and mystics today.

Mysticism, the desire to know God directly, encourages
asceticism as a means of avoiding worldly distraction from
concentration upon the mystic's goal. Asceticism, in turn, is
more easily practiced in seclusion from society. But how
tightly linked are mysticism, asceticism and withdrawal in
different places and eras? Must a mystic be an ascetic too?
Must an ascetic go from self-denial to isolation or to self-
inflicted punishment (rather than stopping at austerity)?
How does self-mortification for religious purposes become
transformed into a spectacle for public entertainment? Is it
possible that a society accustomed to poverty will find
asceticism more congenial than mysticism? If so, might we
find that sufism in Egypt is more ascetic than mystic, at
least among its poorer classes?

Asceticism is interesting in relation to political and economic as well as religious goals.[1] It of course renounces this
world but it can also seek to change it. The proselytizing
sufi orders of centuries ago best exemplify this perhaps con-
tradictory tendency,[2] and this was the viewpoint expressed

---

[1] The social aspects of asceticism have seldom been explored. A good set of
categories from the psychological viewpoint is given by Flugel, pp. 87–94.
[2] See, for example, Birge, p. 27.

to me only recently by 'Rashad Lutfi' (see previous section). Asceticism as a personal habit stemming from religious feeling can be conducive to industry and saving; the many discussions of the historical role of the Protestant ethic make it unnecessary to pursue this point here. But asceticism can lead to productivity if it renounces only the excessive consumption of goods rather than all worldly activity. There is also a congruence between individual asceticism or renunciation of personal wealth and the collective production and accumulation of wealth; they are found together in monastic orders in various religions and in cooperative enclaves based on political or social doctrines (e.g., 'Utopian' communities in various countries, and kibbutzim in Israel).

Sufism glorifies poverty. Using a criterion opposed to the ordinary values, it lends poverty greater prestige than riches. It is a short step from the notion that piety requires poverty to the notion that in general the poor are worthier than the rich or the well off. Asceticism can be related to poverty and wealth in two ways that probably do not exclude one another. First, asceticism may be invoked as a doctrine to combat moral laxity, the corruption of ideals through material abundance. This is the Islamic doctrine of renunciation or abstemiousness (zuhd, the word for asceticism itself). Second, asceticism may be regarded as a useful notion in a poor society; tied to religion and mysticism, asceticism can be invoked to inure people to inevitable hardships, to make acceptable the poverty that they believe (spontaneously or through indoctrination) they cannot eliminate. Here asceticism (zuhd) as a doctrine calls upon and exalts self-restraint, resignation, the capacity to endure suffering, the ability to reduce one's wants or demands upon life. This capacity (ṣabr), though not necessarily connected with religion, makes asceticism easier to follow.

Poverty and excessive materialism are, then, two social

conditions that may be conducive to asceticism; and of course they may occur together in the same society. Early sufi asceticism was somewhat instrumental; the ascetic renounced the pleasures of this world in order to reap a reward in the next one. Later on, the instrumental aspect was abandoned by some thinkers, who stressed that the spiritual state of renunciation is demanded by sufi beliefs irrespective of rewards. Poverty, however, is not an end in itself; rather, it is the route by which one reaches the various stages in the sufi approach to God.[1]

In Egypt today the regime invokes a kind of asceticism by exhorting the masses to refrain from unduly increasing their consumption of goods in order to save for investment in new industry, to reduce the need for foreign exchange, and to help avoid price rises. Individuals are thus urged to curb their desires in the interest of the state and nation. This sort of austerity is different from sufi asceticism, for it is clearly to be temporary and instrumental; the goal is greater material abundance in this life and a more equitable distribution of it among the people. On the other hand, two aspects of political austerity bring it closer to sufi asceticism. First, the regime often couches its exhortations in moral (occasionally verging on religious) terms: Egyptians must produce more while restraining their desire to consume because it is their patriotic duty to do so. Second, spokesmen for the regime sometimes minimize the materialistic motive in order to stimulate idealistic acceptance of the postponed goal: Egyptians should not expect abundance soon—they are working for a better life for their children and grandchildren.

Asceticism based upon religious–mystical motives means low consumption of wealth and a low propensity toward production too. Austerity based upon political and social considerations calls for holding down the rate of increase in

[1] Nicholson, pp. 230–1, quoting Suhrawardi.

consumption but encourages an intense willingness to produce at high efficiency. The regime is thus in the position of discouraging sufism while in another context applauding one of sufism's chief tenets, self-denial. There is also the complicating factor that an increase in wants is essential to the expansion of a domestic market and to economic growth itself.[1] It is clear, however, that the regime has not been able to persuade the masses to curb their desires voluntarily; consumption is kept down, if at all, by a set of restrictive economic policies backed by criminal sanctions, which seems to be the case with other regimes around the world that seek to enforce savings upon an unresponsive population.

Asceticism is in one important sense individual (although men may be ascetics in community): it rewards the individual even if no one else adheres to the practice. Politically-oriented austerity, however, does not produce its reward for the individual unless it is practiced by enough other people to affect the economy. Does this difference have anything to do with the continued success of the religious-ascetic appeal and the wide-spread failure of the political-austerity appeal?

The great issue involving asceticism that William James raised early in this century still remains with us; so we may be excused for momentarily pursuing the subject beyond sufism in Egypt today. It will be recalled that James[2] complained that too large a part of the spirit of his age consisted in the 'worship of material luxury and wealth,' and that children were being raised in excessive tenderness and

---

[1] In the early eighteenth century Mandeville, in his famous *Fable of the Bees*, argued that vice and indulgence are more conducive to wealth than virtue and asceticism (see volume I, last paragraph of the fable, p. 37, F. B. Kaye's commentary on pp. xlvii ff., and Mandeville's Remark F, p. 85, and Remark L, pp. 107 ff.). Yet Mandeville did not on that account call only for indulgence: 'Avarice then and Prodigality are equally necessary to the Society' (Remark Y, p. 250). Though he held luxury to be better for material prosperity, he saw that a civil society had to have other foundations as well.

[2] James, pp. 358–61 (Chapters XIV–XV).

triviality. Seeking a 'bulwark against effeminacy,' he considered war and soldiery to have been effective in this regard, but he rejected war as the 'wholesale organization of irrationality and crime'. So he turned to asceticism or the worship of poverty as 'that moral equivalent of war which we are seeking'. Would not self-denial, he asked, satisfy man's desire for heroism in a constructive way, liberate us from caution and corruption, make us more honest and courageous in the causes we might espouse? In several Western societies today, we are witnessing a rebellion of some young people against established institutions in which the avowed rejection of 'affluence' and the cult of poverty are prominent. It is not, however, a reaction against moral laxity as such or in favor of austerity. It seems instead to rest upon the West's prosperity since World War II and to reject the resulting spread of 'middle class values' to the working class. Rather than seeking to curb desires through a tighter moral code, the rebellion seems to demand at once unlimited freedom for individual expression of feeling and suppression of materialism. So strong is the sense of guilt among many who are materially comfortable that they not only adopt self-denial for themselves but are driven to impose it on others as well. The rebellion shows not sympathy for the poor so much as disappointment that prosperity makes them spiritually no better than the bourgeoisie. The involuntary asceticism of the poor, today's rebels seem to feel, is nobler than anything the poor choose to be when they are able to escape poverty. Perhaps this feeling explains why the rebels appear to be more interested in organizing the poor into a power bloc than in raising their material level of living.

4

Voluntary benevolent societies

The Islamic injunction to give charity has taken several forms. One of the most widespread (yet neglected by scholars) of these forms is the benevolent society with a religious base (jam'īya dīnīya or khairīya). Such associations originated in the nineteenth century, had a rapid growth after World War II and in the late 1950s, and are now being transformed as private contributions decline and governmental support and regulation increase. I shall (1) briefly discuss their historical and legal background, (2) present a selection of data from a Ministry of Social Affairs survey concerning their membership, finances, organization and activity, (3) give some additional material from a more limited Ministry survey of the associations devoted to teaching the Koran, and (4) describe my own observation of the work of several Muslim societies.

HISTORICAL AND LEGAL BACKGROUND

In a brief introduction to its survey of the voluntary associations undertaken in 1960,[1] the Ministry of Social Affairs traced their beginnings to the early nineteenth century and to the increasing complexity of social problems as urban society developed. The survey also mentions foreign examples. By the end of the century there were 65 associations

---

[1] Ministry of Social Affairs, pp. 15–24, 27–9. This survey, used extensively in the following pages, bears no date of publication, but the text (pp. 21, 24, 28–9) indicates that the survey refers to the associations as they were in 1960; the book was probably published in 1963 or 1964.

established which were still in existence in 1960, as table 23 shows.[1] One of these early ones was the Islamic Benevolent Society (al-jam'īya al-khairīya al-Islāmīya,) founded in 1892, in which such prominent figures as Muhammad Abduh and Saad Zaghlul were active. In the 1950s, still important, its president was the political leader Ahmad Lutfi al-Sayyid and among its directors were other personalities of pre-revolutionary Egypt. It had a staff of nearly two hundred full-time, highly-trained social workers and offered educational, medical, and religious services as well as charity to the needy and the aged.[2] Some of the associations founded in the late nineteenth century were also political in nature and secret as well. In the next century, however, the political and benevolent societies, although still called jam'īyat, became increasingly differentiated. The political association was later called a party (ḥizb), and the older term was reserved for the benevolent, and other voluntary associations.[3]

According to the Ministry of Social Affairs, the revolution of 1919 gave rise to more associations as the people developed their own resources and capacities. In this period, two very powerful groups were established: in 1927 the Young Men's Muslim Association (still active), and in 1929 the Muslim Brotherhood, which had great popular influence and until 1954, when it was outlawed, bid for full political power as well. The second quarter of this century, the Ministry points out, saw the opening of social work schools in Alexandria

---

[1] Table 23 must be used with caution. It shows the number of associations *still in existence in 1960* that were established in the indicated time-periods. Especially in the earlier years there must have been associations formed that went out of existence before 1960; these are apparently not included. The survey's historical section (pp. 15–24, 27–9) discusses the development of the associations as if table 23 included all of those formed and dissolved in the various time-periods, or it assumes that all those ever formed were still in existence in 1960.

[2] On this association, see Istiphan, p. 106.

[3] See *E.I.*[2], articles on Djam'iyya and Ḥizb. On the secret political associations, see Landau.

TABLE 23. *Voluntary associations in 1960: location and year of establishment*

Governorate	Before 1900	1900 to 1924	1925 to 1944	1945 to 1949	1950 to 1954	1955 to 1959ᵃ	Not known	Total no.	% of total
Cairo	20	68	240	151	157	399	82	1,117	35
Alexandria	16	52	97	58	59	81	2	365	11
Port Said	5	4	17	13	19	36	4	98	3
Ismailiya	1	2	6	7	6	5	5	32	1
Suez	1	6	11	13	9	24	1	65	2
Damietta	—	1	5	2	5	19	2	34	1
Daqhaliya	5	9	29	24	28	40	9	144	4·4
Sharqiya	3	2	13	18	16	27	10	129	4
Qalyubiya	—	4	15	14	15	20	12	80ᵃ	2·5
Kafr al Shaikh	—	1	6	1	5	10	2	25	0·8
Gharbiya	5	12	29	41	24	28	7	146	4·5
Minoufiya	3	2	22	33	22	23	18	123	4
Buhaira	1	2	15	13	16	35	5	87	3
Giza	—	4	18	18	32	60	6	138	4·3
Beni Suef	1	1	12	9	6	22	16	67	2
Fayoum	2	4	8	14	25	27	—	80	2·5
Minya	1	3	32	19	19	103	7	184	6
Assiut	1	3	20	22	7	27	—	80	2·5
Sohag	—	2	22	14	9	30	—	77	2·5
Qena	—	7	12	14	8	25	13	79	2·5
Aswan	—	3	3	6	6	8	4	30	0·9
Western Desert	—	1	—	1	1	3	—	6	0·2
Sinai	—	2	1	3	2	4	—	12	0·4
Total	65	195	633ᵃ	508ᵃ	496	1,096	205	3,198ᵃ	100
%	2·0	6·0	19·8	15·9	15·5	34·3	6·4	—	100

ᵃ This figure is a correction of or an addition to the one shown in the original source, which is not arithmetically consistent in all details. The changes are negligible in amounts. The total number of associations shown in the table is 3,198, but the survey uses 3,195 in all its other tables, so we use the lower figure, too.

Source: Ministry of Social Affairs, p. 29.

(1936) and Cairo (1937) to supply the trained people needed in the increasing number of benevolent societies. In 1939 the Ministry of Social Affairs was established.

By 1947 Heyworth-Dunne was able to obtain information on 135 associations in these categories: religious, political–religious, social, cooperative, vocational, and charitable. He attributed their growth to (1) the weakening of colonialism following World War II, (2) the feeling among Muslims that they must reject the Western powers that had come close to destroying the world, and (3) the drop in the standard of living after the war and the insensitivity of the ruling classes to the needs of the poor.[1] It was during this period, as the Ministry points out, that the government in 1945 passed the first law specifically regulating the associations and defining their relation to the Ministry of Social Affairs. This law and those that followed, together with the impetus to popular activity supplied by the revolution of 1952 and the establishment of the republic, encouraged a further growth of associations, according to the Ministry's survey. Part of the large increase between 1955 and 1959, especially in Cairo and Alexandria, resulted, the Ministry adds, from the redesignation of government workers' unions as social clubs in accordance with the law of 1956.

Once the government began to regulate associations by specific legislation, its influence became paramount in their development. There have been three main laws since 1945. Thus the government's close regulation of associations antedates the military regime of 1952 but regulation has become tighter under it.

The first broad law dealing specifically with benevolent associations was Law Number 49 of 1945.[2] All associations were required to register in accordance with it. The law

---

[1] Heyworth-Dunne, pp. 27, 30, 50, and pp. 90–1, n. 30.
[2] An English translation is given in Istiphan, pp. 475–7.

stipulated certain kinds of information which the constitution of an association must include; amendments must be approved by the Ministry of Social Affairs. The Ministry was empowered to (1) inspect the finances and to determine if the association's money is spent for its stated purposes, (2) send its representative to ascertain if elections are conducted properly and, if not, to annul them, (3) ask a court to dissolve an association which fails to achieve its purposes, spends its money for purposes other than the approved ones, refuses or gives false information to the government, and violates its own constitution or 'public order' or propriety. Both the Ministry and the association were permitted to appeal the court's decision on the request for dissolution. Finally, associations must have special permission to solicit money from the public. An amendement[1] in 1952 gave the Ministry the right to appoint a temporary board of directors to an association whose regular board lacked a quorum or violated the constitution and rules.

This law clarified the position of associations and enabled them to function in a more orderly way, but it also established firm governmental controls over them. Other laws followed in a similar vein, until codification was made in Law Number 384 of 1956,[2] covering all kinds of associations and foundations: benevolent, welfare, religious (except waqfs), recreational, educational, and scientific. The presidential decree accompanying this law ordered all societies to comply with it or face dissolution, and it specifically ordered the dissolution of the boards and agencies of all welfare associations and their reconstitution in accordance with the new provisions. All societies were permitted now to form branches and to combine in federations. At the same time, instructions were made more specific and binding regarding membership lists,

---

[1] Istiphan, pp. 478–9.
[2] English translation, Istiphan, pp. 483–95.

functions, government inspection, gifts from and affiliation with groups abroad, and investment of funds. The government was to be provided in advance a copy of the agenda of all meetings of the entire membership, might send a representative to such meetings, might invalidate resolutions on subjects not on the agenda, and in emergencies freeze any kind of resolution violating the 'law, public order, or morality'.

With respect to welfare societies particularly, the law permitted the government to combine several in order to co-ordinate their activities, to amalgamate several, to unify the administration of several, and to modify their purposes, all in accordance with the needs of the community as determined by the government. It was provided, however, that in exercising these powers the government should take into consideration the wishes of the founders and the association's goals. Finally, the government was authorized to dismiss directors of the boards of the foundations for various reasons and to cancel any rule of an association's charter.

There was not much more control over the associations left for the government to claim. The accelerated drive toward socialism formed one of the rationalizations for another codification, Law Number 32 of 1964.[1] Now associations were forbidden to conduct more than one broad activity without special governmental approval. Persons who had been deprived of their political rights (for certain political and other crimes) were excluded from associations except by special permission. To function outside the province in which it was located, an association was now required to obtain governmental permission. The Ministry of Social Affairs was authorized to place its representatives on the boards of directors, even to a number exceeding that of the regular members of the boards. Another provision

[1] Arabic text published by Ministry of Social Affairs (Cairo, 1964).

enabled the Ministry to dissolve an association without asking a court to carry out its order. The law also established a fund, controlled by the Ministry, to unify state and private sources of aid to the associations. Finally, it removed the distinctions among types of association insofar as the degree of governmental control was concerned; now the government had uniform and virtually complete control over all of them.

MEMBERSHIPS, FINANCES,
ORGANIZATION, AND ACTIVITY

In its survey of the associations as of 1960, the Ministry of Social Affairs presented a large number of facts, mainly in statistical form. Unfortunately, there is practically no other study of the history and functions of these associations, so that it is not possible to grasp the meaning of all the data in the survey. It is nevertheless useful to have because some of the facts can be interpreted and the survey as a whole can serve as a historical basis of comparison with others that may be undertaken in the future. It would be better if we had previous inquiries with which to compare the results of this one; we do not have any, so we must begin somewhere, and the fact that this is the first comprehensive survey makes 1960 our starting point.

To summarize before going into detail: in 1960 there were in Egypt 3,195 voluntary associations on which the Ministry obtained full information (there were another 520 excluded from the tabulations for various reasons).[1] They had 700,000 members, and had extended, during the year before the survey, a variety of services to perhaps several million persons (exactly how many cannot be determined, as we shall see below) at a total cost of about £E4,000,000. The associations' income in that year was just over £E6,000,000,

---

[1] Ministry of Social Affairs, p. 24.

about a fifth coming from each of these three sources: members' dues, modest fees paid by the beneficiaries of the services, and governmental subsidies.

Only a few of the survey's figures can be checked independently in another study, a directory of the agencies in Cairo in 1955, which includes a few aspects that are also covered in the larger survey. The Cairo directory[1] was compiled by the Social Research Center of the American University in Cairo, with the cooperation of the Ministry of Social Affairs and the two government-supported schools of social work in Cairo. It covered all associations registered in accordance with the law of 1945. The Ministry's survey was made during 1960, and included the associations registered in accordance with the law of 1956, except for those engaged only in sports.[2] Apart from the lapse of five years, it appears that the two sets of data deal with the same categories of associations, except for sports, so that we may reasonably compare the results of each one insofar as the data for Cairo alone are concerned. Up to the end of 1954 the Ministry survey found, as table 23 above shows, 636 associations; to these must be added a certain number of the 82 associations whose date of establishment the Ministry did not discover, and a proportion of the 520 in all Egypt which were omitted from the survey for various reasons. If we calculate these numbers as proportional to Cairo's associations whose year of origin is known and to Cairo's proportion of all Egyptian associations, we should add 222 to the 636 associations the Ministry reported. This figure, however, is considerably smaller than the 1,167 agencies which the Cairo directory found registered with the Ministry.[3] It is doubtful that this

---

[1] Istiphan, p.x.
[2] Ministry of Social Affairs, p. 22.
[3] Istiphan, p. x. Of these 1,167, the Cairo directory says it gives information on about 652; the rest had been dissolved, could not be located, or refused to give information.

difference of over 300 associations can be accounted for by the Ministry's omission of sports associations (which, inspection of the Cairo directory shows, numbered only between twenty-five and thirty in that city, where most Egyptian sports societies are located).

There is another discrepancy, in the opposite direction. The Ministry survey (table 23 above) shows that 157 associations were founded in the period 1950–4, while the Cairo directory shows only 86. According to the Ministry, there were 399 associations established in the period 1955–9; this is the largest increase for any period shown in table 23, and it is unfortunate that we have no independent check upon its accuracy. The Cairo directory data thus suggests that the associations in that city (comprising over a third of those in the entire country) are rather older than the Ministry survey indicates; according to the latter a far greater number were established in the period since the revolution of 1952. The survey, indeed, suggests or states several times that the revolution of 1952 both led to an increase in the rate of formation of the associations and improved the conditions for their establishment and operation.[1] It is relevant, therefore, to note here that the Cairo directory was compiled on the basis of actual visits to the associations' offices, whereas it is at best not clear that the Ministry survey involved such visits.[2]

The Cairo directory permits us to make another calculation that is not possible by using the Ministry's survey; this is the specific religious basis of the associations. Since people frequently—perhaps usually—refer to them as religious associations (jam'īyāt dīnīya), it is surprising that the survey does not present among its many tabulations one showing how many associations are Muslim, Christian, Jewish, and non-sectarian. It does, however, list 'religious services'

---

[1] Ministry of Social Affairs, pp. 12, 18, 28.
[2] Istiphan, p. x, and Ministry of Social Affairs, pp. 21–3.

among all others extended by the associations, but does not identify these services by the specific religion itself, as we shall see below. In its summary and conclusions, the survey says that the associations have made a great contribution to the religious and cultural life of the nation, and then characteristically goes on to speak of socialism as the animating principle behind such popular activity.[1] The Cairo directory, however, by giving the names, specific activities, policies, and membership requirements of the associations, enables us to estimate their religious affiliation. Of the 649 Cairo associations listed in 1955–6, nearly 250 were clearly Muslim in inspiration or entirely Muslim in membership, 190 Christian, and 14 Jewish. In the other 200 or so, religion was either unclear or irrelevant. It is likely that the proportion of Muslim associations is greater than this in all other parts of the country except Alexandria. (Except for religious services, of course, the associations usually extend their help irrespective of the religion of the beneficiaries. People habitually go for all kinds of services to associations of their own religious group, but no medical clinic, for example, would refuse to help someone of a different religion.)

Table 24 shows that in 1960 there were about 700,000 members, over three quarters of them men and about the same proportion of both sexes active to the point of paying dues regularly. Thus 2·7 per cent of the 26 million Egyptians were members of these associations, a proportion somewhat lower than that found in countries with a higher standard of living and educational achievement, but probably higher than would be found in most countries at Egypt's stage of development. Dues-paying members constitute half or more of the total membership in 2,446 associations, or 77 per cent of the total number.[2] The average number of members per

---

[1] Ministry of Social Affairs, p. 197 and p. 194.
[2] Ministry of Social Affairs, p. 47 (second table).

7-2

TABLE 24. *Voluntary associations, 1960: membership and dues payment, by sex*

Sex	No. of members	Members paying regular dues	
		No.	%
Male	642,700	503,098	78
Female	57,280	46,907	82
Total	699,980	550,005	78

Source: Ministry of Social Affairs, p. 47.

TABLE 25. *Voluntary associations, 1960: size of membership*

No. of members	No. of associations	% of total
Less than 50	719	23
50–199	1,501	47
200–499	586	17
500–999	167	5
1,000 and over	99	3
Not reported	123	4
Total	3,195	100

Source: Ministry of Social Affairs, extracted from table, p. 56.

association is 219, but, as table 25 shows, most have fewer than 200 members. Of the 99 associations with 1,000 or more members, 64 are in Cairo and seven in Alexandria.[1] Cairo has by far the largest proportion of the total membership, just half. Alexandria, second in rank, is far behind with only 11 per cent; no other city or province has more than 5 per cent of the members.[2] In the large cities, too, the associations have the highest ratio to the population; put another way, these cities—Cairo, Alexandria, Port Said, and Suez—have the smallest population per association, making

[1] Ministry of Social Affairs, table, p. 56.
[2] Ministry of Social Affairs, table, p. 50.

them probably the best served by the associations. Their average population per association is only about 3,100, whereas the average for other areas ranges from 8,500 to 20,000 (with one as high as 39,000).[1]

The survey, in its own evaluation, found it disappointing that only 2·7 per cent of the population were members of the associations, and called for greater efforts to persuade people to join them and to play their part in the socialist society.[2]

Another indication of how active the members are appears in table 26,which shows that a fifth of the associations held no general membership meeting in the previous year. Of those that did, just over half reported an attendance rate of 50 per cent or better.

In its conclusions, the survey drew special attention to the place of women in the associations. This is not surprising, for the role of women in welfare work has become increasingly prominent, and the survey itself was published during the tenure of a woman minister, Egypt's first woman to achieve cabinet rank. Table 24 above shows that 57,280 women were members of the associations, constituting only 8 per cent of the total number, although a larger proportion among them than men were dues-paying members. Among all the associations, the vast majority, over two thirds, were limited to men, whereas only 135, or 4 per cent, were exclusively women's organizations. Of the 836 mixed societies, consituting a quarter of the total, 755 had male majorities and only 81 female majorities. The survey claimed that the mixed associations have been more successful, but it offered neither criteria nor evidence. The survey offered these reasons for what it regarded as the low proportion of women: vestiges of tradition (presumably meaning Islamic practice, though this was not specified); a lower degree of education; and the

---

[1] Ministry of Social Affairs, table, p. 31.
[2] Ministry of Social Affairs, pp. 193–4.

TABLE 26. *Voluntary associations, 1960:*
attendance at annual meetings

Annual meeting	Number associations	% of total
No meeting held	652	20
Meeting held, proportion present		
less than 20%	460[a]	14
20–49%	443	14
50–74%	844	27
75% and over	763	24
Not reported	33	1
Total	3,195	100

[a] This is a correction of the total shown in the source.
Source: Ministry of Social Affairs, abstracted from table on p. 64.

traces of capitalism, a system that encourages 'passivity' in women.[1]

The income of the associations closely follows size of membership. Total income in 1960 was £E6,044,489. With 50 per cent of all members, Cairo associations had 46 per cent of all income. Alexandria, with only 11 per cent of the membership, had 20 per cent of the income. Thus these two cities alone had two thirds of all income; no other city or province had more than 5 per cent, or about £E290,000.[2] Table 27 shows income from all sources for the country as a whole and for those governorates with at least one hundred associations. For all Egypt, about a fifth of the associations' income comes from each of these three sources: members' dues, government contributions, and small fees that beneficiaries pay to clinics, schools and so on. There are some oddities that we do not have enough information to explain. The province of Minoufiya, for example, derives 21 per cent of its income from its property, as against a national average of

[1] Ministry of Social Affairs, p. 194.
[2] Ministry of Social Affairs, p. 131.

TABLE 27. *Voluntary associations, 1960: income from various sources for all governorates and for those with at least 100 associations (in Egyptian pounds)*

Governorates	No. of associa- tions	Membership dues		Government contributions		Private gifts and contributions[a]	
		Amount	%	Amount	%	Amount	%
Cairo	1,117	653,437	23·5	632,053	22·7	258,049	9·2
Alexandria	365	147,291	12·3	171,375	14·3	112,039	9·3
Daqhaliya	144	26,044	17·5	37,538	25·3	19,941	13·4
Sharqiya	129	137,308	66·1	12,760	6·1	11,161	5·3
Gharbiya	146	31,485	16·1	24,503	12·5	33,207	16·9
Minoufiya	123	10,934	12·3	19,356	21·8	5,216	1·4
Giza	138	91,017	54·3	22,415	13·3	4,396	2·6
Minya	184	17,448	18·5	23,298	24·8	11,725	12·4
Total U.A.R.[d]	3,195	1,316,866	21·8	1,203,708	19·9	632,611	10·6

Governorates	No. of associa- tions	Fees for services		Proceeds from sales[b]		Income from property	
		Amount	%	Amount	%	Amount	%
Cairo	1,117	535,616	19·3	48,846	1·8	209,244	7·5
Alexandria	365	352,847	29·5	84,176	7·0	122,632	10·3
Daqhaliya	144	34,245	23·0	3,121	2·1	12,186	8·2
Sharqiya	129	20,312	9·8	3,530	1·7	3,488	1·7
Gharbiya	146	64,016	32·6	2,524	1·3	13,003	6·6
Minoufiya	123	5,711	6·4	4,414	5·0	18,770	21·1
Giza	138	20,133	12·0	7,023	4·1	1,567	0·9
Minya	184	8,903	9·4	1,593	1·6	1,538	1·6
Total U.A.R.[d]	3,195	1,185,767	19·6	176,563	3·0	438,946	7·3

Governorates	No. of associa- tions	Public appeals[c]		Other		Total income	
		Amount	%	Amount	%	Amount	%
Cairo	1,117	229,180	8·2	213,921	7·6	2,780,346	100
Alexandria	365	89,218	7·5	125,132	10·5	1,194,710	100
Daqhaliya	144	7,160	4·8	8,380	5·6	148,615	100
Sharqiya	129	13,258	6·4	5,970	2·9	207,745	100
Gharbiya	146	20,643	10·5	6,761	3·5	196,142	100
Minoufiya	123	15,286	17·2	9,323	10·4	88,909	100
Giza	138	13,201	7·8	7,797	4·6	167,549	100
Minya	184	27,911	29·6	1,680	1·8	94,096	100
Total U.A.R.[d]	3,195	510,830	8·3	579,198	9·5	6,044,489	100

Source: Ministry of Social Affairs, adapted from table on unnumbered insert following p. 140.

[a] Includes contributions from private individuals in Egypt, contributions from abroad, private and organizational gifts for specific purposes, and contributions in kind.
[b] Sales of articles produced in workshops and training centres.
[c] Includes lotteries.
[d] Includes all governorates, not only those shown in the table; hence the total at the bottom does not equal the sum of the preceding figures in the column.

TABLE 28. *Voluntary associations, 1960: amount
of governmental subsidies*

Amount (£E)	Associations	
	No.	%
Nothing	2,374	74·3
1–24	80	2·5
25–49	74	2·3
50–99	101	3·2
100–199	104	3·3
200–499	169	5·3
500–999	114	3·5
1,000 and over	172	5·4
Not reported	7	0·2
Total	3,195	100·0

Source: Ministry of Social Affairs, constructed from chart on unnumbered page following p. 132.

only 7 per cent. It also derives a relatively large proportion, 17 per cent, from public appeals and lotteries, compared with a national average of only 8 per cent; Minya derives an even larger proportion from this source, about 30 per cent. Gharbiya receives a third of its income in fees for services, Sharqiya two thirds from members' dues.

The extent to which the associations are self-supporting may be shown by the proportion of their income from dues, fees, contributions, and so on, or simply by what we may take to be the reciprocal of this support, that is, the extent to which they receive governmental subsidies. Table 28 shows that three quarters of the associations received no subsidies at all in 1960, and that only a seventh received £E 200 or more annually. The total amount the government distributed, table 27 shows, was £E 1·2 million, of which about half went to Cairo. These sums came from the budgets of the Ministries of Social Affairs, Education, and Waqfs, and from the Governorate of Cairo. Large subsidies to a few associations

Voluntary benevolent societies

TABLE 29. *Voluntary associations, 1960: proportion of income derived from governmental subsidies*

Proportion of income	Associations	
	No.	%
None	2,379	74.5
1–9%	181	5.6
10–19	129	4.1
20–29	107	3.4
30–49	131	4.1
50–74	150	4.7
75% and over	111	3.4
Not reported	7	0.2
Total	3,195	100.0

Source: Ministry of Social Affairs, constructed from chart on unnumbered page following p. 132.

must have accounted for most of these governmental grants, for, as table 29 shows, these grants formed a substantial proportion of the income of only a few associations. Thus only 392 associations received from the government 30 per cent or more of their income. They comprise only an eighth of all associations, but they comprise nearly a half of the 809 receiving subsidies of any size. Thus when the government gives a subsidy at all, it tends to be an important one in relation to the independent income of the association that gets it. Apparently the government has decided to concentrate its support among a few agencies instead of spreading it among many. One of the criteria in deciding which associations to support appears to be the quality of the services rendered. In its conclusions, the survey proposes an increase in government aid, which, it adds, must be based on this criterion. The need for an increase in subsidies, the survey points out, is emphasized by the fear that economic conditions might affect the level of private contributions.[1] This remark,

[1] Ministry of Social Affairs, p. 198.

TABLE 30. *Voluntary associations, 1960: expenditures for all governorates and for those with at least 100 associations (in Egyptian pounds)*

Governorate	No. of associations	Administration		Main services		Aid in kind	
		Amount	%	Amount	%	Amount	%
Cairo	1,117	1,198,679	39·2	1,290,152	42·2	51,613	1·6
Alexandria	365	535,750	51·6	390,025	37·5	16,446	1·6
Daqhaliya	144	84,012	56·8	44,707	30·2	2,244	1·5
Sharqiya	129	47,189	27·1	112,147	64·4	63	—
Gharbiya	146	69,374	36·0	89,840	46·6	3,500	1·8
Minoufiya	123	32,971	39·2	24,176	28·8	4,442	5·3
Giza	138	58,257	36·0	81,739	50·5	5,761	3·5
Minya	184	43,602	47·1	35,993	38·8	78	0·1
Total U.A.R.[c]	3,195	2,414,240	42·2	2,359,918	41·0	110,789	2·0

Governorate	No. of associations	Donations for limited purposes[a]		Workshops[b]		Maintenance of property	
		Amount	%	Amount	%	Amount	%
Cairo	1,117	45,116	1·5	50,274	1·6	173,552	5·7
Alexandria	365	1,709	0·1	14,715	1·4	24,147	2·3
Daqhaliya	144	2,578	1·7	7,361	4·9	2,732	1·8
Sharqiya	129	74	—	3,795	2·1	5	—
Gharbiya	146	4,628	2·4	4,560	2·4	3,035	1·5
Minoufiya	123	7,852	9·3	6,005	7·1	2,118	2·5
Giza	138	1,597	0·9	4,596	2·8	190	0·1
Minya	184	250	0·3	4,929	5·3	4,407	4·7
Total U.A.R.[c]	3,195	71,050	1·2	148,305	2·5	224,952	4·0

Governorate	No. of associations	Public appeals and lotteries		Other		Total expenditure	
		Amount	%	Amount	%	Amount	%
Cairo	1,117	47,034	1·5	201,351	6·5	3,057,771	100
Alexandria	365	7,523	0·1	47,901	4·6	1,038,216	100
Daqhaliya	144	2,055	1·3	2,174	1·5	147,863	100
Sharqiya	129	272	0·2	10,398	6·0	173,943	100
Gharbiya	146	7,781	4·0	10,032	5·2	192,750	100
Minoufiya	123	1,098	1·3	5,346	6·4	84,008	100
Giza	138	1,091	0·6	8,593	5·3	161,824	100
Minya	184	1,541	1·7	1,738	1·7	92,538	100
Total U.A.R.[c]	3,195	75,312	1·3	338,273	5·8	5,742,839	100

[a] Not further explained.
[b] Cost of producing articles sold for income.
[c] Includes all governorates, not only those shown in the table; hence the total at the bottom does not equal the sum of the preceding figures in the column.

Source: Ministry of Social Affairs, extracted from table, p. 140.

relevant to the situation before 1960, is even more pointed in view of the extensive nationalization of private property and the ceiling on earnings imposed well before the publication of the survey. It is an interesting question, but one on which there is no documentary evidence, whether the associations have more or less money now that the government has increased its control and its subsidies. The idea keeps emerging that the religious obligation of alms-giving (zakāt) should become part of the secular tax law at a fixed rate; this revenue the government would then distribute to the public and private welfare agencies. Such an outcry regularly follows this suggestion that it has never come close to adoption.

How the associations spend their income is shown in table 30. They disburse a total of £E5·7 million, compared with an income of just over £E6 million. The largest proportion, over two fifths, goes for administration, and another two fifths goes for the main services (I shall return to both categories). All other classes of expenses are very small. As in the case of income, here, too, there are several oddities that we cannot explain in the present state of information. Administrative costs, for example, are particularly high in Alexandria, whereas in Sharqiya they are especially low while the proportion going for the main services is very high.

The figures on income and expenditure show that most of the associations are very small indeed, receiving and disbursing only a few pounds. Table 25 above showed that nearly a quarter of the associations had fewer than fifty members and over two thirds had fewer than 200 members. Now we can see in table 31 that over two fifths of the societies had an annual income and outlay of less than 200 pounds; that is, their transactions amounted to appreciably less than an average of $1·25 daily on each side of the ledger. The

TABLE 31. *Voluntary associations, 1960: income and expenditures (in Egyptian pounds)*

Amount	Income		Expenditures	
	No. of associations	% of total	No. of associations	% of total
Less than 50	477	14·9	483	15·1
50–99	384	12·0	385	12·0
100–199	486	15·2	486	15·2
200–499	589	18·4	587	18·4
500–999	396	12·4	765	23·0
1,000–1,999	348	10·9	—	—
2,000–4,999	286	8·9	289	9·0
5,000 and over	226	7·0	229	7·2
Not reported	3	—	1	—
Total	3,195	99·7	3,195	99·9

Source: Ministry of Social Affairs, adapted from table on p. 143.

TABLE 32. *Voluntary associations, 1960: size of deficits (in Egyptian pounds)*

Amount of deficit	No. of associations	% of total with deficits
1–24	380	33·9
25–49	128	11·4
50–99	142	12·7
100–199	147	13·1
200–499	171	15·3
500–999	84	7·5
1,000 and over	68	6·1
Total	1,120	100·0

Source: Ministry of Social Affairs, extracted from second table, p. 176.

total cash balance of all associations was £E 2·85 million, or about half of total expenditures and nearly half of income. But the balances of a large proportion were very small, in accordance with their low income and outlay; thus 37 per cent had a balance of less than £E 50.[1] Many also operated

[1] Ministry of Social Affairs, table, p. 188.

Voluntary benevolent societies

TABLE 33. *Voluntary associations, 1960: geographical extent of services*

Extent	No. of associations	% of total[a]
Entire country	326	10·2
Entire governorate (province)[b]	1,197	37·5
Capital city of a governorate	311	9·7
Sub-region of a governorate[c]	127	3·9
Capital city of a sub-region	229	7·2
City district[d]	267	8·4
Village	594	18·6
Not reported	144	4·5
Total	3,195	100·0

[a] Small percentage corrections of the original table have been made.
[b] Muḥāfiẓa.   [c] Markaz.   [d] Qism.
Source: Ministry of Social Affairs, adapted from table, p. 32.

with a deficit. There were 1,120 that did so, or a little over a third of all associations. Table 32 shows that of these a third were very small deficits amounting to less than £E25 for the year. Yet, because of the low income of so many societies, these deficits, small as they were in pounds, were an appreciable burden in relation to income; thus nearly half of the associations with a deficit had one that amounted to more than a fifth of income.[1]

We can now look more closely at the objective of the associations' activity and finances, that is, the services they provide. Table 33 shows that, at least in intent, nearly two fifths serve the entire governorate (i.e., province—the very large cities are also provinces) in which they are located. As the survey points out,[2] villages are not well served by the associations, which are mainly urban; almost certainly the largest, most active and most effective ones are located in the urban centers.

Specific services, amounts spent on each, and the number

[1] Ministry of Social Affairs, first table, p. 176.
[2] Ministry of Social Affairs, p. 33.

TABLE 34. *Voluntary associations, 1960: expenditure on services, and beneficiaries*

Type of service	Expenditure		Beneficiaries	
	Amount (£E)	%	No.[a]	%
Medical, health	1,242,100	31·3	4,568,361	31·4
Cash assistance	840,042	21·2	711,611	4·9
Cultural, educational	726,508	18·3	948,621	6·5
Religious	314,010	7·9	7,176,484	49·4
Child care	297,170	7·5	73,024	0·5
Sports, amusements	173,656	4·4	354,533	2·4
Vocational training	124,741	3·1	19,012	0·1
Vocational training for handicapped	63,243	1·6	16,364	0·1
Care of delinquent and homeless minors	51,248	1·3	4,448	0·1
Care of aged, beggars	27,546	0·7	914	—
Rural services	22,003	0·6	344,445	2·4
Leadership training	17,289	0·4	3,935	—
Maternity care	3,687	0·1	139,673	1·0
Research and studies	3,511	0·1	—	—
Alcohol, drugs	620	0·1	13,894	0·1
Other	57,080	1·4	152,779	1·1
Total	3,964,454	100·0	14,529,098	100·0

[a] For some services, these numbers do not refer to individual persons.

Source: Ministry of Social Affairs, extracted from table, p. 82.

of beneficiaries, are shown in table 34. Nearly a third of the expenditure goes for medical and health services, about a fifth for cash welfare payments, and nearly another fifth for education and culture (most of this category is taken up by schools). Of the remaining services, only religious and child care approach substantial amounts, and the rest are very small. Thus, medical care, cash payments, schools, religious activities, and child care account for nearly nine tenths of the nearly £E4 million spent on services.[1] The number of benefi-

[1] Table 34 shows nearly £E4 million going for services, but table 30 above shows only £E2·4 million for the 'main services'. This discrepancy, probably due to calculation of different elements, is not explained in the survey.

ciaries of those services presents a more complicated problem. The total number shown in table 34 is 14·5 million persons but, as the survey itself implied,[1] when one person made several visits to a clinic for treatment of one ailment, such visits were counted as services to several individuals; a similar difficulty, the survey says, arose in enumerating the individual persons benefiting from religious, cultural and educational services.

These services are extended to the public at a rather high administrative cost to the associations, as the survey itself mentions.[2] As table 30 above shows, £E2·4 million of the total expenditure of £E5·7 million, amounting to 42 per cent, goes for administration. It is not clear why these costs are so high. The associations in 1960 had 12,417 full-time and part-time employees, who received total annual wages of £E1·7 million, amounting to about 70 per cent of all administrative costs.[3] There are also many unpaid volunteers. We simply do not have enough background information to assess these figures, but we shall return to their implications for the quality of the services extended to the public.

Since we are especially interested in the religious basis and activities of the associations, we shall consider the few figures in the survey relating to these services. Table 34 shows that religious services, though accounting for only 8 per cent of the associations' total outlay of money, was fifth in order of the actual amount spent on the sixteen kinds of service shown. More important, however, is the indication that the beneficiaries of religious services far outnumber those of any other service; indeed, they constitute nearly half of the 14·5 million beneficiaries of all services together. This is significant even if we deflate the number because it

[1] Ministry of Social Affairs, p. 84.
[2] Ministry of Social Affairs, pp. 16–17.
[3] Ministry of Social Affairs, p. 65, and table, p. 68.

TABLE 35. *Voluntary associations, 1960: expenditures for religious services, and beneficiaries (in Egyptian pounds)*

Governorate	Amount	% of total spent in governorate	No. of beneficiaries
Cairo	61,541	3·6	4,333,514
Alexandria	73,938	7·5	1,222,247
Port Said	5,371	4·6	61,819
Ismailiya	2,924	15·7	76,019
Suez	5,064	13·4	3,767
Damietta	1,232	5·6	9,202
Daqhaliya	22,472	15·7	27,089
Sharqiya	55,293	43·1	74,409
Qalyubiya	8,152	17·9	139,427
Kafr al Shaikh	2391	15·9	1,314
Gharbiya	16,780	10·3	81,033
Minoufiya	7,311	13·5	96,942
Buhaira	10,386	12·9	270,741
Beni Suef	3,160	10·2	11,675
Fayoum	3,518	20·9	8,522
Minya	6,413	9·6	18,555
Assiut	3,518	3·4	95,142
Sohag	5,271	11·1	23,794
Qena	6,738	9·0	180,429
Aswan	664	4·7	1,257
Sinai	1,564	36·4	1,567
Western Desert	629	9·0	218
Total	314,000	7·9	7,176,484

Source: Ministry of Social Affairs, extracted from tables, pp. 95, 82.

must include multiple visits to mosques, for example, by one person, and so on. It is all the more a pity, as I have already mentioned, that the survey does not tell us more about these services and about the religious basis of the associations.

Table 35 shows virtually everything else the survey tells us about religious services. Here again there are wide differences in the proportions spent by the various governorates which we have no way of explaining at present. The data were apparently collected on different systems from place to place; thus it is peculiar that Suez should have spent more than Assiut and yet have fewer than 4,000 beneficiaries against Assiut's 95,000.

Among the associations providing these religious services, the survey tells us,[1] are those especially devoted to teaching children to memorize the Koran (taḥfīẓ al-Qur'ān); they have various names, but together they are called Associations for the Preservation of the Koran (jam'īyāt al-muḥāfaẓa 'alā al-Qur'ān). The survey tells us little more about them, but in 1964 they were the subject of a special (unpublished) report by the Ministry of Social Affairs, which I shall summarize.[2]

The report found 291 Koran associations in Egypt, 55 per cent of them in villages. In some of these villages, this kind of society was the only welfare group found. Affiliated with these associations were 388 branch agencies distributed as follows: 237 for teaching memorization of the Koran, 70 educational agencies, 42 mosques, 21 libraries, 8 vocational training centers, 5 nurseries, and 5 athletic clubs. The 291 parent associations had 26,470 members, of whom only 203 were women; in most provinces the average membership per association was less than one hundred. Members in good standing, who paid dues regularly, constituted 71 per cent of all members. In the year previous to the report, 143,139 persons benefited from the activities of these associations; the report does not say how this figure was obtained and whether or not it includes multiple services to individual persons.

To these facts should be added relevant information from other sources. First, the survey of mosques discussed in Chapter 2 above reports that in 1962 there were 1,000 out of 2,997 governmental mosques with sections for teaching the memorization of the Koran; they had 23,247 pupils.[3] Some of these mosques were probably affiliated to the associations

---

[1] Ministry of Social Affairs, p. 94.
[2] The data on these associations come from this unpublished report: 'Associations for the Preservation of the Koran.'
[3] Ministry of Waqfs 1963, table, p. 143.

discussed in the special report I am summarizing, but the documents themselves give no indication one way or the other. Second, in the early 1960s the government recorded and published forty-four discs containing the entire chanted Koran, and then broadcast them regularly on an exclusive wavelength of the state radio.[1]

The income of the 291 Koran associations in the year preceding the report was £E 140,064, of which two fifths came from governmental subsidies. They spent £E 131,040 in the same year, of which 71 per cent went for programs and services, and 29 per cent for administration. The services, despite the name of the associations, are not mainly religious. Ninety-nine per cent of the outlay, in fact, went for a combination of services of which religion was only one element; the others were general education, cash assistance, vocational training, recreation, and medical and health care. Other services included athletics, nurseries for children, and care of the blind. The report says (without explaining how the figure is obtained) that the average cost per beneficiary of all services was 60 piasters (about $1·40). The highest average cost per person was a little over £E 7 (about $16·40), for vocational training. The next highest was £E 2·5 (about $5·65), for children's nurseries. The average for religious services, including teaching the Koran, was 50 piasters (about $1·15); this seems low, but it may be the result of large classes with consequent small unit cost. The report gives no other average costs per person, so we cannot tell how religion fares except in relation to the services already mentioned.

The report found that the 291 associations had a total of 1,646 officials and workers, of whom all but 161 were full-time, receiving a total of £E 74,400 in wages for the year. (This is much more than the £E 38,239 the report says went

---

[1] The conception and execution of this project are described by its originator, Al-Saʿīd, pp. 83 ff.

for administration but this question is not discussed in it.) As for the educational qualifications of these employees, only 7 per cent (113) were fully qualified, 36 per cent had some qualifications, and 57 per cent had no qualifications at all. It is clear, therefore, that the 113 fully qualified workers were not numerous enough to provide even an average of one qualified worker for each of the 291 associations.

The report on the Koran associations reached these conclusions. First, they were not limited to instruction in the Koran but extended to a wide range of welfare service, primarily relating to family and child care whether through education, vocational training, cash aid, and so on. Second, the teaching of the Koran was mainly accomplished not through regular educational institutions but rather as part of the functions of welfare societies and, in any case, involved mostly children of pre-school age. Third, as organizations, they revealed irregularities. Some held membership meetings in violation of their constitutions, and others failed to hold such meetings, likewise a violation. Fourth, the associations suffered from a shortage of full-time help, especially of qualified persons; salaries, also, were too low. Fifth, the quality of service was not high enough. Finally, administrative costs, at 29 per cent, should have been no higher than 20 per cent.

In view of the work and limitations of the associations, the report made the following recommendations (which, like the conclusions just reported, are scattered through the report; I have brought them together here). First, in accordance with Law Number 32 of 1964, the Koran associations should be redefined, their objectives and services made more consistent with one another, and their overlapping work coordinated. Second, the organization and operation of the associations should be improved through raising the professional level of their welfare services, raising the level and pay of employees, and increased assistance of various kinds (including subsidies) from the Ministry of Social Affairs. Third, the services of the societies deserve to be better known and more intensively used, especially in the rural areas. Finally, the mosque should be better used as a religious and cultural institution with functions relating also to the social conditions of the people in its area; to this end, the imams must be better trained.

Thus the Koran associations have been extending services rather like those of the other voluntary associations I have been describing. The quality of both types has not been satisfactory to the Ministry of Social Affairs. I have already indicated that most of the associations have a small number of members, many of whom are not active, that their budgets are very small and their administrative costs high. One official in the Ministry told me that a couple of hundred agencies in Cairo—coordinated, properly staffed and financed—could do the work better than the thousand or more then operating. On another occasion, however, the same official, not thinking of his earlier remark, said that many of the clinics and hospitals that the government had taken over from voluntary associations were giving much poorer service because they now received no private funds and the government was unable or unwilling to support them on the previous scale, and the spirit of spontaneity and service declined considerably under government operation. Over-crowding and neglect were the main complaints.

Undoubtedly, the work of the associations can be improved, and very likely the Ministry of Social Affairs could supply the talent needed to raise the level of the services offered by the associations. The question is, nevertheless, whether the form that government assistance has taken could have preserved the special quality of these voluntary agencies. I was told by many leaders of the associations as well as by some Ministry officials, that the general level of services declined as the government took them over or assisted in them. Many of the agencies welcomed government aid of various sorts, realizing they needed it. But such aid was given with little imagination and not much respect for the achievements of the associations, which had been carrying out these functions before the government took so great an interest in them. Although this interest, on the part of many officials, was genuinely directed toward needed improvements in the work of the associations, much of it has been ideologically inspired in recent years. The survey itself, for example, emphasizes the associations' relevance to socialism while playing down their religious impulse. In its conclusions, the survey praises them as the autonomous creations of citizens who feel a responsibility to help solve social problems. While recognizing the value of such free endeavors, however, the survey immediately adds that the 'socialist conception of the new society demands of us a certain limitation of that freedom, a channeling, which is essential to the planning of welfare programs'. Its statements and tone suggest that coordination or limitation is a value in itself, and that, in any form, it contributes to the public good.[1] The position, as it was explained to me in principle by the Minister of Social Affairs in late 1964, was that the government sought to persuade the agencies to shift from religion to social welfare, which itself was a noble Islamic goal. Though private support was declining, the associations themselves, now increasingly supported by the government, were not declining. The government's policy, the Minister pointed out, was to assume full responsibility for those welfare needs that became national in scope; thus the private associations initiated services and identified needs which, when they became national and the associations showed that the needs could be met, the government stepped in to take over. In this domain, too, it

[1] Ministry of Social Affairs, p. 193.

appears that the government, instead of doing things that the private agencies do not do, prefers to take over the tasks they perform fairly well.

As to regulation (rather than take-over), recent laws, summarized above, impose a large number of requirements that the leaders and officials of the associations have found oppressive. They gave me numerous examples of rules that even the Ministry did not mind seeing ignored or violated; most frequently these examples told of the manufacture of reports of meetings that never took place but which were required by laws designed not to improve the conduct of the associations but to facilitate governmental surveillance or, perhaps even worse, merely to satisfy a bureaucratic passion for regulation. The associations, also, have been drawn into the wide net by which the regime seeks to maintain its influence; thus government officials inquired of many associations in the spring of 1968 whether they had held discussions of the 30 March speech of the President of the Republic (made in response to the unusual open and serious political criticism), which workers in factories and offices were gathered to discuss. The program (the subject of a referendum a few weeks later) and these discussions were fully covered in the daily press (all government-owned).

During the fall of 1964 and the spring of 1965, I visited a variety of the associations. All of them were religious-based and Muslim. Although I was aware of the many important Coptic and other Christian societies, as well as of the Jewish ones now reduced in number and activity with the great shrinkage of that community since 1947, I was mainly interested in the Muslim ones as part of this study of the predominant religious institutions in Egypt. I saw some societies whose services were conducted humanely, imaginatively and efficiently and some whose work was far inferior. The ones I visited regularly in Cairo were far better than the average;

among them I have selected six to describe briefly in order to show something specific of the nature of these societies. These six, therefore, are certainly not 'typical' of all associations, nor even, perhaps, of the better ones. They are, I believe, typical of the impulse and intention of the people who came together in these societies and who continue to support them in difficult times.

The most traditional of these six societies is the Shar'īya Cooperative Society of Followers of the Koran and the Sunna of Muhammad.[1] Its headquarters building and mosque are in the low-income, working-class district of Darb al-Ahmar. Founded in 1913 by the well-known Shaikh Mahmoud Muhammad Khattab al-Sibky (1858–1933), it was later headed by his son. When I visited it, the association had 2,800 members paying annual dues from $1·40 to $2·80; most of them were workers, merchants and government employees. The members of the governing board were all officials or teachers in the religious establishment of the Ministry of Waqfs or Al-Azhar. The headquarters conducted the mosque and daily religious lectures, and some of the association's hundred or so branches (about half outside of Cairo) ran clinics too. The leaders are traditional in general outlook, and middle-class in status; the beneficiaries, however, are generally very poor. The leaders are active men, quick to appreciate the outsider's interest and to insist on the perfection of Islam even when it was not the issue.

Somewhat more modern is the Islamic Association for Moral Character, in Rod el Farag, a district that is mainly working-class but with lower middle-class groups including tradesmen, lower-level government workers, and people

---

[1] Istiphan's *Directory of Social Agencies* in Cairo gives information on five of the six associations. It gives this one's name in English as Al-Shar'ia Association for the Followers of the Koran and the Mohammedan Sunna (al-jam'īya al-shar'īya li ta'āwun al-'āmilīn bil-kitāb wa-l sunna al-Muḥammadīya). Istiphan, p. 185. The word shar'īya refers to Islamic religious law; sunna refers to the practices and precepts of the Prophet and his Companions.

from the countryside. This association was founded in 1895.[1]
Its chief services have been educational and religious, with
five schools and two mosques. More than two thousand
pupils attend its schools; pupils used to pay fees but when
compulsory education was introduced in Egypt the association abolished fees in exchange for government subsidies.
The association also publishes a magazine containing articles
on religion, and gives charity. In 1965 it had about a hundred
and fifty members, most of them workers and tradesmen,
paying annual dues ranging from $1·40 to about $7. Members
of the board of directors, however, were middle-level government officials, teachers, and merchants; the president had
higher education and headed a state-owned company. A few
spoke English, which they had learned in school. The board
and general membership dressed in Western clothing. The
schools were run on modern principles and were orderly and
well maintained. In the members of the association one
immediately saw a genuine faith directed toward communal
action, social improvement and concern for the poor. Many
members thus volunteered a great deal of their spare time to
help the sizable paid staff.

The Islamic Educational Society[2] is newer than the two
groups just described, having been established in 1944. One
of the more successful ones, the society conducts a mosque;
a free school for boys six to fourteen years old, in which the
regular state curriculum is supplemented by memorization
and study of the Koran to prepare the best ones for Al-
Azhar institutes; a Koran evening school and lectures for
adults; and a clinic. The society has a well-kept building and
mosque in Shubra, a rather mixed area in which some sec-

[1] Jam'īyat makārim al-akhlāq al-Islāmīya. Istiphan gives 1897 as the year of
establishment, my notes show 1895, and certain of the society's documents
indicate Muḥarram 1317 A.H., which would put it in 1899.
[2] Jamā'at al-tarbīya al-Islāmīya. A summary of this organization appears in
Istiphan, p. 109, where its name is translated as Islamic Cultural Group.

tions have a high proportion of Christian residents and where there are many upper-level working class and middle-income families. The society provided space, also, for the headquarters of a local unit of the Arab Socialist Union; I was told that this was not so much an ideological move as a way of helping the neighborhood people to obtain municipal services and other kinds of governmental assistance somewhat like, it appeared, the kind provided by urban political machines in America.

Members, paying annual dues from $1·40 to $2·30, were mainly tradesmen and lower-level government officials. The board, however, had people of greater influence. The head was Shaikh Ali Al-Mansouri, a well-known religious leader in the district and an occasional writer on religious subjects. Several board members were active or retired government officials of the third or fourth rank. Two others were building contractors in private enterprise; another was the head of the Arab Socialist Union in a nearby district.

The society's classrooms were lively yet orderly. I also attended sessions of Koranic commentary (tafsīr) under Shaikh Ali's leadership. On one such occasion he covered verses 100 to 150 of the fourth chapter entitled 'Women' (sūrat al-nisā'), asking many questions of his audience of a dozen men; they all readily responded and listened raptly to the shaikh's own explanations, many of which he made looking directly at me in honor of the guest. I attended some public lectures following the evening prayer. A typical one was given by a shaikh in the administration of Al-Azhar. Dressed in Eastern style, he sat on a chair in front of the mosque's pulpit (minbar), a floor microphone before him. His theme was that Islam is a religion for all of humanity, not only for Arabs; but it is not enough to believe, he emphasized—we must also live as the Prophet lived, helping our fellow man. The speaker had no text before him. He spoke forcefully, explaining, pleading, cajoling and exhorting; he laughed and almost cried, demanded and proclaimed, even scolded and admonished, as he gestured with his body, his head, shoulders and arms, his eyes, hands and fingers. The audience was responsive, some even enthusiastic. There were about seventy-five people, including five women and girls and about thirty-five boys from the school. Half the men were dressed in Western clothing, the other half in some-what shabby Eastern clothing. When the speaker had taken his audience through a gamut of emotional states for forty minutes, he concluded on an ascending note, whereupon many men rushed up to him, shook and kissed his hand, his turban ('imma) and his shoulder.

The youngest of these associations was the Abū Bakr al-Ṣiddīq Society,[1] founded in 1952 in Heliopolis, in a distinctly middle-class district. The founders were eight friends, two of them civil servants, two merchants, two army officers, one laborer, and one middle-level employee in the accounts de-partment of a Western company operating in the Middle East. The idea for the association came to the last-named and a friend while they were performing the evening prayer in a mosque during Ramadan; they saw the need to help the working class families living in or near middle-class neighbor-hoods in this half-century old suburb of Cairo. The members are largely of middle income and pay annual dues of about $2·80. The association absorbs the full energies of a small number of unpaid leaders as well as a considerable amount of time of many members. They are all religious but rather modern in general outlook; they wear Western clothing, and many speak English well. Some of the leaders criticized two types of people: those, like members of sufi orders whose extreme piety blinds them to social needs, and others who,

[1] Mu'assasat Abī Bakr al-Ṣiddīq, named for the first caliph. Istiphan, p. 6.

concerned with secular power, are interested in politics and think that the lives of the poor can be improved that way.

The association conducts a mosque, sponsors evening lectures on religious subjects for adults, a trade school for girls, two medical clinics, and a combination nursery and school for children under six years of age.

The trade school teaches sewing, embroidery and rug-making to girls twelve to sixteen years of age who could not go beyond primary school, are not trained for any job, and whose families are poor. Instead of going into domestic service or simply remaining idle, they attend classes all day for two years, following which they get factory jobs, or work at home, or get married. The school is located in a well-designed building in an open, clean neighborhood; it is supervised by a trained woman, and the girls are taught by pleasant, expert teachers. The atmosphere is wholesome, friendly and family-like. The staff are conscientious, patient and kind. Eager to impress the visitor, they tend sometimes to put too much emphasis on the things the girls produce and not enough on the relationships among them and between them and the staff.

One of the society's clinics was located in the same group of sturdy buildings with the mosque, trade school and nursery, in the middle-class neighborhood. It was clean, modern and pleasant, and well staffed—but with few patients and a big deficit. It had been established to help the local people of middling incomes, from $60 to $90 monthly; such families, however, preferred to go to private doctors. This clinic, charging about twenty-five cents per visit, was left with only a few servants who worked in the neighborhood. Another clinic, a few minutes away in the society's original headquarters, was in the center of several poor neighborhoods. Charging only a bit more than a dime per visit, and serving a more populated and poorer area, this clinic was always busy. From its regular and special fees, the clinic covered all its expenses. The quality of medical care in both clinics was high. They were fairly cheerful places, with conscientious doctors, nurses and servants, and had much less than the usual institutional gloom of clinics.

The nursery-school was at the society's headquarters, occupying a tree-shaded building with several well-furnished classrooms, and a playground. The children, all from the neighborhood, were mostly four and five years old but a few were as young as three. They attended classes from eight until twelve-thirty on four mornings, and on two mornings only until eleven. They were all bright, active but orderly, and were well-behaved in and out of class. During recess they were allowed to play freely in the yard; occasionally, the old caretaker (perhaps to enforce discipline in the presence of a visitor) slapped a child who was slow to respond to his commands for more decorum. Once I saw the old shaikh who taught the children to memorize the Koran restrain him gently as he was about to slap a child who was slow to get in line to return to class. There were two other teachers, both competent and devoted young women. In Koran class, the children were able to recite a few verses. The shaikh proudly pointed out a Coptic girl reciting with the others, adding that there were one or two more in the school and that it was not inappropriate because the Koran was intended and helpful for all persons, not merely for Muslims. They also recited a nationalistic poem and a verse extolling the President of the Republic, whose photograph on a large poster was on every classroom wall. The children knew the sounds of the letters one teacher put on the blackboard and could read simple words formed of the sounds familiar to them. The other young woman taught the children to read numbers, emphasizing the difference, for example, between 14 and 41, which apparently causes some difficulty for Arab children as well as foreign adults learning Arabic.

Voluntary benevolent societies

I visited two contrasting women's societies. The Moslem Ladies Club at Sayyida Zainab,[1] founded in 1937, is the more traditional of the two. Located in a mixed district of low-income families, its several hundred members, paying minimum annual dues of about $2·75, were mostly women who had completed secondary school. Few of them had careers outside their homes; many were married to professional men. They were more modern and independent than average women, but many of them still wore rather modest Western clothing: long black dresses and coats, and veils over their heads (but not covering their faces). Articulate, intelligent, and competent, the leaders and staff were dedicated to their work, which they related very closely to religion. The society conducted daily public lectures at several mosques, discussion groups for members in private homes, charity, a four-year vocational training course for about thirty girls aged eight to fourteen, and hostels for girls attending both the association's schools and others. All of these enterprises were well run by a competent paid staff and ardent volunteers. On one occasion I was somewhat surprised to see, at a public lecture, a small audience of a dozen elderly women dressed in black, with veils covering their heads. The thirty-five minute talk by an elderly shaikh dealt in a simple way with some highly theoretical questions in Islam. There was a wall poster with an excerpt from the National Charter. The women seemed cheerless, wrapped up in their own thoughts rather than attending to much that the speaker said. I myself could not see much in his rambling talk that touched his dejected audience, but at the end they appeared happy enough with the experience.

The other ladies' club, the Islamic Women's Society (Jamāʻat Nisāʼ al-Islām), was established in 1957, deliberately

---

[1] Jamāʻat al-sayyidāt al-Muslimāt bi-l Sayyida Zainab, which the Cairo directory translates as Moslem Women's Group at Sayyida Zainab. Istiphan, p. 148.

on Y.W.C.A. lines. This is a distinctly upper middle-class group comparable to many in the West. Its well-educated members, many of whom speak English well, pay annual dues of $2·30. Many of them follow independent careers as doctors, lawyers and teachers. The society conducts hostels for about a hundred Arab young women from abroad attending Egyptian universities, lectures on religious subjects, a professional family counseling bureau, and also gives charity. The articulate and active leaders give a faintly feminist impression. One of their main goals, aside from the ordinary one of lifting the social level of women, is to raise standards of women's education in order to make them better wives to educated men.

5

The place of government

At several points I have contrasted the sufi order with the voluntary association. Although they both stem from religious attitudes, their differences are more significant than their broad similarity. The following summary of these contrasts (in nature if not always in practice) may be useful.

Nature and characteristics	Sufi order	Voluntary association
Approach to religion	(1) 'Traditional' (2) Appeals to diffuse religious feelings: God, worship, the beyond	(1) 'Modern' (2) Tries to meet specific urban needs: charity, education, medical care
Activities	Almost exclusively religious: prayer, fasting, contemplation, ritual	Partly religious, but through other main activities: schools, lectures, clinics
Participants' goals	Related to self and to members exclusively	Members exalt selves through aid to non-members
Benefits conferred	Exclusively spiritual and personal	Spiritual, but through material aid of social character
Relation to government	(1) Jurisdiction in Ministry of Interior (2) No subsidies	(1) Jurisdiction in Ministry of Social Affairs (2) Subsidies

In discussing religious behavior and institutions in Egypt today through statistical surveys and my personal observations of mosque organization, sufi orders and voluntary associations, I am aware that much has been left out and much that has been included has been unexplained. I have felt it useful to present this information, even if we cannot assess all of it, because the subject needs the attention of scholars. It is likely that religious organization in Egypt is at, or has just passed, a critical point. If the institutions I have discussed manage to survive, then this discussion will have provided at least some basis for comparison with their later forms. If, as some people in Egypt told me they expect, they do not survive, then we shall have at least some idea of their nature before their disappearance or transformation.

The danger to religious autonomy in Egypt does not lie in the advent of secularism. The religious establishment has long ceased to aspire to real political control; it has accepted secularism in fact if not in principle. But because religious beliefs and loyalties continue so strong among the people, the avowedly secular holders of power are themselves unwilling to be fully secular even though they proclaim themselves socialists and revolutionaries. Controlling all the nation's institutions, it is they who connect religion with politics by using it in domestic and international affairs. There are undoubtedly some religious leaders who would like to exercise more influence in the state, but nowadays they can neither do so nor even express such an idea. The military regime's denial of political influence to the 'ulamā is not secularism, for (1) this denial extends to every elite or popular body that might reduce the regime's total sway, and (2) the 'ulamā and religious bodies are denied not only political influence but even autonomy in religion itself. Secularism means separation of church and state and the latter's supremacy; it does not call for the state's control of the intimate details of religious teaching or the harnessing of religion to the purposes of the government of the day.

In some cases the regime (as we have seen in Chapter 2 on the mosques) associates itself with religious organization and sentiment. A significant example of this policy, in a time of adversity, occurred in a major speech by the President of the Republic shortly after the loss of territory to Israel in June 1967. On 23 July, the anniversary of the regime's assumption of power, he said that despite all its achievements the revolution faced its greatest crisis. He told the nation that perhaps Almighty God wanted to test it to judge whether it deserved its achievements; that perhaps God also wanted to teach the nation a lesson, to purify it as it proceeded to build the 'new society'. Whatever the Almighty's will might be, he added, the nation accepted the test as its destiny. Pointing out that he had personally and correctly informed the military commanders that Israel would attack on 5 June, he told the nation that their leaders knew what was coming but could not prevent defeat. The President than took refuge in a popular saying that he recalled to the nation: Precaution is useless against fate (Lā yughnī ḥadhar 'an qadar).[1]

In other cases, as in that of the voluntary associations, the government takes pains to minimize their religious basis and to put them to other ideological uses. In its conclusions to the survey of associations the Ministry of Social Affairs stated: 'In view of the importance of this activity in shaping the human being, elevating his moral conduct, and in developing his relations with others on the basis of cooperation, solidarity and love, it behooves us to study ways to increase the capacity of these associations to create social consciousness and to spread the enlightened spirit of socialism among the masses.'[2]

The military regime's nervous intervention in the associational life of the people parallels its action regarding autonomous political and economic influence. Following a Near Eastern tradition, it has repeatedly chosen to emphasize

[1] Text in *Al-Ahram* (Cairo), 24 July 1967, p. 3, columns 1 and 5; translated in Laqueur, pp. 199, 203.
[2] Ministry of Social Affairs, p. 197.

control rather than to encourage incentives and spontaneity. It sees certain popular activities doing some good; seeking to enhance them, the regime has increasingly regulated or appropriated these activities, thus reducing both the usefulness of the work and the autonomy of the popular groups themselves. To contribute their best to society, individuals and groups need from government (1) general conditions of justice, order and security, (2) guarantees that private power shall not prevail over the public interest, and (3) in the case of popular associations, special conditions such as licensing and registration, protection of rule by members, assistance in providing trained workers, help in studying needs and methods of meeting them, and so on. Too often in the Near East and elsewhere, governmental power has overwhelmed individuals and non-political groups. The effect of excessive state power is usually wider and more devastating than that of excessive private power. If, as I have argued, it is characteristic of *Islam* that it should produce many voluntary associations for social and religious ends, it may be characteristic of the *Near East* that government should aim so persistently to control such associations and that they should soon succumb to political power.

Yet, in the recent popular Egyptian response to military defeat, there may be a renewal of associational independence. The judiciary are not precisely the sort of association I have been discussing, but their action in the spring of 1968 may have some bearing on the future of voluntary societies. Taking seriously the injunction to think about change during such a critical time, the judiciary, meeting as a professional society, issued a statement that both pointed to the need for autonomy and presented to all Egyptians an unusual example of it. The statement, submitted to the President of the Republic, stressed the need to insure the independence of the bench and of the state's attorneys in the investigation of crimes; it also pointed out (perhaps in an allusion to military officers in judicial roles), that only qualified persons should be judges in court. On more general matters, the judiciary asserted: 'It is necessary to insure for every citizen personal liberty of thought, speech and assembly, of participation in criticism, controversy [ḥiwār] and suggestion, and of the feeling of responsibility and power in free expression. This is not possible except by the affirmation of the rule of law, which means above all the guarantee of liberties to all citizens and the supremacy of the law over the rulers as well as the ruled.' And to make it clear that they were not uttering acceptable platitudes, they took this stand: 'Men of the judiciary and the state's attorneys, for their part, believe that in order to preserve the independence of the judiciary and to guarantee justice, they must all completely refrain from participating in any political arrangement of the Socialist Union at any level.'[1]

[1] Judiciary of the United Arab Republic, pp. 4, 8. It did not take very long for the regime to respond to this display of independence. In 1969 a series of Presidential decrees overhauled the judicial system. (They were published in the official gazette, *Al-jarīda al-rasmīya*, No. 35b, 31 August 1969, pp. 678–82; No. 36, 4 September 1969, pp. 683–726; No. 36b, 10 September 1969, pp. 729–32.) All judicial appointments and promotions were placed in the immediate control of the President. The Minister of Justice was replaced by another. Many members of the judiciary were retired or transferred to other ministries. The judicial association, which issued the statement summarized above, was reorganized under new leadership.

Sources

This is simply a list of the works cited briefly in footnotes to the text. It is not intended as a guide to further reading on the subjects of this book, although some of the works mentioned can serve that purpose.

Abdul Rauf, Muhammad. 'Some Notes on the Qur'anic Use of the Terms Islām and Imān,' *The Muslim World*, **57**, 94–102 (1967).

Abun-Nasr, J. M. *The Tijaniyya. A Sufi Order in the Modern World* (London, 1965).

Al-Saʿīd, Labīb. *Al-muṣḥaf al-murattal* (*The Chanted Recitation of the Koran*) (Cairo, 1967).

Al-Ṭawīl, Tawfīq. *Al-taṣawwuf fī Miṣr* (*Sufism in Egypt*) (Cairo, no date, probably 1946).

'Associations for the Preservation of the Koran,' Ministry of Social Affairs, United Arab Republic, unpublished report, 4 pp. Cairo, 1964).

Baer, Gabriel. *A History of Landownership in Modern Egypt 1800–1950* (London, 1962).

Baer, Gabriel. *Egyptian Guilds in Modern Times* (Jerusalem, 1964).

Birge, John K. *The Bektashi Order of Dervishes* (London and Hartford, Conn., 1937).

Crecelius, Daniel. 'Al-Azhar in the Revolution,' *The Middle East Journal*, **20**, 31–49 (1966).

Depont, Octave, and Xavier Coppolani. *Les Confréries Religieuses Musulmanes* (Algiers, 1897).

E.I.[2] *Encyclopedia of Islam. New Edition* (Leiden and London, 1960–).

El-Shayyal, Gamal El-Din. 'Some Aspects of Intellectual and Social Life in Eighteenth-Century Egypt,' in P. M. Holt, ed.,

Sources

Social and Political Change in Modern Egypt, pp. 117–32 (London, 1968).

Evans-Pritchard, E. E. *The Sanusi of Cyrenaica* (Oxford, 1949).

Flugel, J. C. *Man, Morals and Society* (New York, 1945).

Gibb, H. A. R. *Mohammedanism. An Historical Survey* (London 1949).

Gibb, H. A. R., and Harold Bowen. *Islamic Society and the West* (London, 1957), Volume I, Part Two.

Gilsenan, M. D. 'Some Factors in the Decline of the Sufi Orders in Modern Egypt,' *The Muslim World,* **67,** 11–18 (1967).

Goldziher, I. *Le Dogme et la Loi de l'Islam* (1910), tr. Félix Arin (Paris 1920, 1958).

Gramlich, Richard. *Die Schiitischen Derwischorden Persiens. Erster Teil: Die Affiliationen* (Wiesbaden, 1965).

Heyworth-Dunne, J. *Religious and Political Trends in Modern Egypt* (Washington, D.C. 1950).

Ḥusain, 'Alī Ṣāfī. *Al-adab al-ṣūfī fī Miṣr fī-l qurn al-sābi' al-hijrī (Sufi Literature in Egypt in the Seventh Century of the Muslim Era)* (Cairo, 1964).

Ibn Manẓūr. *Lisān al-'Arab (The Arabic Language)* volume 9 (Bulaq, Cairo, 20 volumes, 1883–90).

Istiphan, Isis. *Directory of Social Agencies,* Social Research Center of the American University in Cairo (Cairo, 1956).

James, William. *The Varieties of Religious Experience* (1902) (Modern Library edition, New York, various dates).

Judiciary of the United Arab Republic. 'Statement and Resolutions of the General Meeting of the Judiciary of the United Arab Republic Convened at Their Club in Cairo, 28 March 1968' (in Arabic), *Majallat al-quḍāh (Journal of the Judiciary)*, volume 1, no. 2 (special number), pp. 1–8.

Kahle, Paul. 'Zur Organisation der Derwischorden in Egypten,' *Der Islam,* **6,** 149–69 (1916).

Sources

Khadduri, Majid, and Herbert J. Liebesny, eds. *Law in the Middle East,* volume I (Washington, D.C. 1955).

Kissling, H. J. 'The Sociological and Educational Role of the Dervish Orders in the Ottoman Empire,' *Studies in Islamic Cultural History* (ed. G. E. von Grunebaum), American Anthropological Association, Memoir No. 76, April 1954, pp. 23–34.

Landau, Jacob M. 'Prolegomena to a Study of Secret Societies in Modern Egypt,' *Middle Eastern Studies,* I, 1–52 (1965).

Lane, Edward. *The Manners and Customs of the Modern Egyptians* (1836) (Everyman's Library edition, London, 1944).

Lapidus, Ira M. *Muslim Cities of the Later Middle Ages* (Cambridge, Massachusetts, 1967).

Laqueur, Walter, ed. *The Israel–Arab Reader. A Documentary History of the Middle East Conflict* (New York, 1969).

Lewis, Bernard. 'Islamic Guilds,' *The Economic History Review,* **8**, 20–37 (1937).

Lewis, Bernard. *The Emergence of Modern Turkey* (London, 1961).

Macdonald, Duncan B. *Aspects of Islam* (New York, 1911).

Mandeville, Bernard. *The Fable of the Bees* (1705, 1714). Commentary by F. B. Kaye, 2 volumes (Oxford, 1924).

McPherson, J. W. *The Moulids of Egypt* (Cairo, 1941).

Meier, F. 'Soufisme et Déclin Culturel,' in R. Brunschvig and G. E. von Grunebaum, eds. *Classicisme et Déclin Culturel dans l'Histoire de l'Islam* (Paris, 1957).

Ministry of Social Affairs, United Arab Republic. *Taqwīm al-jamʿīyat wa-l muʾassasāt al-ijtimāʿīya* (*Survey of Associations and Organizations*) (Cairo, no date, probably 1964).

Ministry of Waqfs, United Arab Republic. *Al-istithmārāt* (*Investments*) (Cairo, no date, probably 1964).

Ministry of Waqfs (1963), United Arab Republic. *Al-masājid. Bayānāt iḥṣāʾīya ʿan al-masājid allatī tushrif ʿalayhā wiẓārat al-*

awqāf fi-l jumhūrīya al-ʿarabīya al-muttaḥida (The Mosque. Statistical Report on Mosques Supervised by the Ministry of Waqfs in the United Arab Republic) (Cairo, 1963).

Ministry of Waqfs (1964*a*), United Arab Republic. *Al-masājid. Bayānāt iḥṣāʾīya ʿan al-masājid al-ahlīya fi-l jumhūrīya al-ʿarabīya al-muttaḥida. (The Mosques. Statistical Report on Private Mosques in the United Arab Republic)* (Cairo, 1964).

Ministry of Waqfs (1964*b*), United Arab Republic. *Wizārat al-awqāf fī ithnā ʿashara ʿāmman, 1952–64 (The Ministry of Waqfs During Twelve Years, 1952–64)* (Cairo, 1964).

Moriah, Gabriel. *The Social Structure of the Sufi Associations in Egypt in the 18th Century* (Unpublished Ph.D. thesis, University of London, June 1963).

Mubārak, ʿAlī. *Al-khiṭaṭ al-tawfīqīya al-jadīda li Miṣr al-Qāhira (Topography of Cairo and Egypt)*, 20 volumes in 4. (Cairo, 1887–9).

Nicholson, Reynold A. *A Literary History of the Arabs* (Cambridge, 1907, 1953).

Rahman, Fazlur. *Islam* (London, 1966).

Sanhoury, A. *Le Califat* (Paris, 1926).

Sanitation Committee for Mosque Improvement, Ministry of Waqfs, Government of Egypt. *Taqrīr lajnat al-handasa al-ṣiḥḥīya li-l nuhūḍ bi-l masājid (Report of the Sanitation Committee for Mosque Improvement)* (Cairo, 1942).

Shaltūt, Maḥmūd. *Al-fatāwā (Legal Opinions)* (Cairo, no date, probably 1964).

Shorter E.I. Shorter Encyclopedia of Islam. H. A. R. Gibb and J. H. Kramers, eds. (Ithaca, New York, 1953).

Smith, Margaret. *Studies in Early Mysticism in the Near and Middle East* (London, 1931).

Taftazānī, Abū-l Wafā al-Ghunaimī. ʿAl-ṭuruq al-ṣūfīya fī Miṣr,ʾ Cairo University, *Bulletin of the Faculty of Arts*, **25** (Part II): 55–84 (1963) (published in 1968).

ʿUlwān, Muḥammad Maḥmūd. *Al-taṣawwuf al-Islāmī (Islamic*

Sources

Sufism), The General Administration of the Sufi Orders
(Al-mashyakha al-'āmma li-l ṭuruq al-ṣūfīya) (Cairo, 1958).

'Uweis, Sayyid. *Min malāmiḥ al-mujtama' al-Miṣrī al-mu'āṣir.
Ẓāhira irsāl al-rasā'il ilā ḍarīḥ al-Imām al-Shāfi'ī (Some Charac-
teristics of Contemporary Egyptian Society. The Phenomenon of
Sending Letters to the Tomb of the Imam al-Shāfi'ī.)* National
Center of Social and Criminological Research (Cairo, 1965).

Weber, Max. *The Sociology of Religion,* tr. Ephraim Fischoff
(Boston, 1964).

Wehr, Hans. *A Dictionary of Modern Arabic,* ed. J. Milton
Cowan (Ithaca, New York, 1961).

Zwemer, Samuel. *Heirs of the Prophets* (Chicago, 1946).

Index

In aphabetizing, this index ignores the Arabic article, al.

Index

Mosques (*cont.*)
  Improvement, 13–15; as voluntary association, 7; worshippers in, 13
Muezzin (mosque official), 11, 37–44
Muhammad Ali, 69
Muslim Brotherhood, 71, 91
Mysticism, 84–5

Nicholson, Reynard A., 64

Qāri' (mosque official), 11–13, 37–44

Religion: autonomy, 128; governmental policy toward, 44–9, 53–61, 80–1; popular and official, 4, 73–6, revival of, 76–9; study of, 1–2; *see also* Islam

Ṣabr, 86
Sanhoury, A., 8
Sanitation Commission for Mosque Improvement, 13–15, 45, 54,
Secularization, 1, 128–30
Sufism and sufi orders: appeal, 73–80; asceticism and mysticism, 84–9; charges of degeneration, 71–2; compared with voluntary association, 127; governmental policy towards, 72, 80–1; 'high' and 'low', 76–7; khalwa, 83–4; mawlid, 81–3; and 'modernization', 80; opposition to, 78–80; orders in Egypt, 67–8; organizational structure, 67–72; origin and nature, 63–4, 74–5; and orthodoxy, 64–5;

Ottoman era, 70; paradoxical aspects, 66–7; political decline, 70–1; rebelliousness, 66; revival of, 76–8; shaikh (leader), 68–70; and state, 65; study of, 62, 64, 76
Supreme Council for Islamic Affairs, 47–50
Supreme Sufi Council, 67–8, 70–2, 80

'Ulamā, 9, 128
United Arab Republic, *see* Egypt

Virgin Mary, vision of in 1968, 73
Voluntary associations, 7; in Mamluk era, 7–8; loss of autonomy, 8; *see also* Voluntary benevolent societies
Voluntary benevolent societies: administrative costs, 111; autonomy, 128–31; compared with sufi orders, 127; examples of, 118–26; finances, 102–9; governmental policy towards, 105, 107; legal status, 93–6; membership, 99–101; origin and growth, 90–2; religious aspects, 98–9, 111–16, 129; services to public, 109–13; statistical summary, 96–7; women in, 101–2, 125–6

Waqfs, 17, 50; *see also* Ministry of Waqfs

Zuhd, 86

138